S0-AXR-997

HOW TO FIGHT BACK AND WIN

HOW TO
FIGHT BACK AND WIN
The Joy of Self-Defense

JUDITH FEIN, Ph.D.

Torrance Publishing Co.

© 1996. 2002 by Judith Fein

Torrance Publishing Company
P.O. Box 2558
Sebastopol. CA 95473
Phone or FAX (707) 823-3581

First Edition
3rd Printing. September 2002, Revised
4th Printing. September 2004

Printed in the United States of America

Library of Congress Cataloging-in Publication Data

Fein. Judith
    How To Fight Back and Win

    Includes index
    1. Self-Defense. 2. Self-Defense for Women.
    3. Rape—Prevention.

I. Title
Library of Congress Catalog Card Number: 95-060721
ISBN: 0-929523-28-8

Cover Art: "Women Triumphant" © Nancy Worthington
Cover Design: Jack and Donna Fisher-Communication
            Graphics
            Photographs: Nancy Worthington
Photograph—back cover: Kathleen Higuera
Copy Editor: Donna Fisher

*This book is dedicated to L. Duck and to D. Van Duck
who embody and exemplify the spirit
of joy, freedom, and triumph.*

CONTENTS

PREFACE

I wrote *How to Fight Back and Win* to complement *Exploding the Myth of Self-Defense.* While *Exploding the Myth...* is the philosophy behind self-defense and personal power, *How to Fight Back and Win* is the *nuts and bolts* guide which teaches individuals the practical aspects of exactly how to successfully fight back and win. Although both books are complete in and of themselves, together they form a greater whole. The many success stories of *Exploding the Myth...* give inspiration to those wishing to learn self-defense and take control of their lives.

One unique aspect of *How to Fight Back and Win* is the way I organized the book. Instead of separating physical skills into one section and preventive and psychological techniques into another, I chose to write each chapter as a lesson; the totality of the book becomes a course in self-defense. I wrote as I actually teach my classes. Therefore, the reader can either be actually taking a course in self-defense or be studying at home—almost as if being present as one of my students.

An interesting side note is how the title was chosen. I developed four titles. Almost as a joke, I added *The Joy of Self-Defense* as a subtitle to *How to Fight Back and Win.* I then surveyed approximately 125 people. To my great surprise, *How to Fight Back and Win—The Joy of Self-Defense* won by a landslide. The *joy of self-defense* is a wonderful concept whose time has come. It implies freedom and power and happiness in being in control of our lives.

I asked artist Nancy Worthington to create an original work of art for the cover. She created "Women Triumphant." And there you have it: power, joy, and triumph—the message of this book!

ACKNOWLEDGMENTS

I would like to express my thanks to my students at San Francisco State University and San Francisco City College for providing me with the feedback which was so necessary to keep this project moving along. I wish to especially thank the following individuals who formed the self-defense class found on page 19 of this book: Alyssa Dineen, Michelle Womack, Cayetana Bujor, Taryan Dethlefs, Jeannie Gant, Sherine Ta, Britt Schlosshardt, Mak Kegelmeyer, Loretta Chietti, Karin Cotterman, Mary Ann Aban, Lacy MacCombs, Brigitte Ann Robbins, Tammy Huynh, and Renate Gilkyson. Many thanks go to Lori Rillera and Jean Green for their stories.

Thank you to Gregg Morris who graciously acted the part of the assailant for the photographs in this book and to Todd Trujillo, who stood in as a second assailant. Gregg is the Head Tennis Professional at Montecito Heights Health and Racquet Club in Santa Rosa, California. (We discussed posting Figure 58 with the caption "You *will* win the tennis match!") Special thanks go to Catherine DuBay, the general manager of Montecito Heights, for her support and for giving us acccess to the club for photo sessions.

Thank you to Kathleen Higuera for the excellent back cover photo. A very warm note of thanks goes to artist Nancy Worthington, who created an original artwork for the cover of this book and also took the excellent inside photographs. Finally, I especially wish to thank my editor, Jean Gilliam, for her expertise in English grammar and her promptness.

LESSON ONE
An Overview

"Something happened the other day when I was waiting for the bus, but I don't know if it was a success story because I didn't physically hit anyone."

"What happened?"

"I was standing at the bus stop. A man came from the other side of the street. I could tell from the look in his eyes that something was wrong. He rushed at me and started screaming that he was going to kill me because I was standing in his space. I got in my [karate] stance, clenched my fists, looked him straight in the eyes and angrily yelled at him that I was going to break every bone in his face! Just before he reached me he veered off and ran in another direction."

I asked members of my self-defense class how many of them thought that this was a success story. Every hand in the room went up.

Understanding This Book

How To Fight Back and Win is written for you, as if you were present, participating in a series of self-defense classes. *How To Fight Back and Win* is written as a course on self-defense. Each chapter is a separate lesson presented in the same sequence as I teach my own classes. Since I have divided the book into a series of lessons, topics proceed in sequence. Lessons on physical fighting skills are interspersed with assault prevention and personal safety topics.

Introductions

Why are you taking this class in self-defense? (Remember, this book is a self-defense course, whether you are reading it in your own home, or enrolled in a formal class.) Over the years, I have received many answers. Earlier answers ranged from "I needed an extra credit" to "This is the first time I am living on my own and I am interested in learning how to take care of myself." Now, when I ask this same question, I get a totally different set of answers. I rarely hear the extra credit response. Current responses are more like these. "I work late and walk home alone on deserted streets. I want to learn how to take care of myself." "I hear about so many horrible things happening. I want to be prepared." "I think that self-defense is a necessity. I wish this class was taught in elementary school." "I plan on travelling by myself and want to feel safe." "I take mass transportation at night. I want to be prepared, just in case anything happens." "I don't want to feel afraid anymore. I want to be in control of my life."

Self-Defense Skills as Survival Skills

Self-defense training must be thought of as survival training. You do this in the same vein as CPR or lifesaving.

The skills you learn are those that will help you know what to do in a crisis, and how to act accordingly. You learn what works, what doesn't work, and why. Through knowledge and training you become able to control the situation, thus making appropriate choices.

The Myth of Self-Defense

The myth of self-defense is that the enemy on which we are focusing our defense is outside of ourselves. When our concerns focus on rapists/muggers/intruders/kidnappers/carjackers/street harassers, etc., we are not in control of the situation. The real enemy is within us. The real enemy is a

Figure 1. Self-Defense Class

combination of our own social conditioning, and our fear. For a comprehensive explanation and discussion on the *myth of self-defense*, read Chapters One and Ten, Exploding the Myth of Self-Defense in *Exploding The Myth of Self-Defense—A Survival Guide for Every Woman.* (Fein—Torrance Publishing)

The Joy of Self-Defense

Self-defense begins with self-esteem. The psychology of self-protection starts with a fundamental belief in your own worth as a human being. In order to fight back and win, you must not only like yourself, you must learn to love and believe in yourself. This love and self-respect needs to be nurtured so that it can grow. You are special; you are unique. No one has the right to hurt you.

The point of power comes from within us. Personal power is our control over our own lives. If we are to be in control, then we must take responsibility for our choices and our actions. If we blame another person or the society for our problems and our lack of control, then we give up our power and, by definition, are powerless. When we tap into our own sense of power, then we, and not the assailant, make the decisions.

Therefore, when we change our focus from the external enemy to ourselves and learn the tools of empowerment, we conquer the enemy within. We become powerful. We have control. Self-defense becomes a joy when we feel powerful. When we feel afraid, our lives are self-limiting. We get battered around and feel out of control. When we have power and control, we direct the course of our own destiny. We make our own choices and run our lives the way we see fit.

The joy in self-defense comes from knowing that you have options—that you can take care of yourself—that you are your own person. No one can take your power away from you. No one had better try to hurt you. If anyone does, he will be sorry that he was ever born!

The Fear of Fighting

As a result of societal conditioning, combined with a lack of experience and participation in contact and/or competitive sports, women in general have fears about fighting back. Most women have never really struck anyone in self-defense, and many women have never been struck. For your own preservation (psychologically as well as physically), it is necessary to physically hurt someone who is attacking you. In fact, in many cases, you will need to incapacitate him.

Common fears expressed are:

"I am afraid that I will freeze—that I will try to scream and that nothing will come out."

"I am afraid that I will hit him but won't hurt him."

"I am afraid of big men because I am small."

"I am afraid to get him angry."

"I am afraid that if I try to fight back I will get killed."

"I am afraid to fight because I might get hurt."

"I am afraid to hurt anyone."

"I am afraid that I will get too angry and lose control."

At the very beginning of these lessons, it is proper to discuss the concept of the fear of fighting. Keeping these fears prevents a woman from becoming powerful and fighting back successfully. We will address these fears in LESSON THREE: How to Win—The Psychology of Fighting Back.

The Three Levels of Defense

Think of self-defense in terms of keeping distance between you and someone who wants to harm you. You can conceptualize this strategy in terms of placing barriers between you and the assailant. The barriers can be physical or psychological or both. Figure 2. is a simple diagram designed to help you understand the three levels of defense. Notice the arrows between Prevention and Psychological and between Physical and Psychological. These levels are interconnected— with the Psychological being the connecting thread.

Prevention

Prevention is your first line of defense. If you can prevent an assailant from getting to you, then you don't have to go through the nasty business of getting rid of him. Prevention can be thought of in terms of (1) mechanical security and (2) personal safety awareness habits.

Mechanical security

Mechanical security simply means devices. These devices are designed to deny entry, to alert you so that you are not taken by surprise, or to keep intruders away. Common devices are locks, lighting, and alarms. Locks and security systems will not do you a bit of good if you fail to use them. Therefore, good safety awareness habits become tantamount.

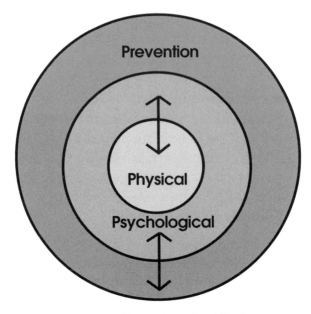

Figure 2. The Three Levels of Defense

Personal safety awareness

Good safety awareness habits go further than locking doors and setting your alarm system. They involve a knowledge of what assailants do and of how to psychologically, as well as physically, prevent a criminal from even getting close. (We will discuss this concept more when we address the topics of home safety and street safety.)

The Psychological

I firmly believe that self-defense is at least seventy-five percent psychological. It is imperative that we gain a thorough knowledge of assailants' patterns. We must know what they do and how they do it. We must also learn how to prevent an assailant from approaching us, what to do if one does, and how to get rid of him very quickly—usually within three seconds.

We must also understand the differences between victim and resister behavior and learn how to become a resister. These topics will be discussed in the chapter on psychological skills.

Physical Defense

Physical defense is your last line of resistance. You need it when the preventive and psychological barriers have been breached. Knowing and being able to skillfully apply physical self-defense techniques are extremely important. Knowing that you are skilled in physical defense will enable you to move with confidence—thus enhancing your psychological and preventive skills. Physical skills will enable you to easily incapacitate an assailant—which you must do if you are either being attacked or being seriously threatened with bodily injury. Physical skills will also enable you to break out of holds and grabs. In short, a thorough knowledge of physical skills may help you get away safely and may save your life. Please note that psychological skills are always utilized at the same time as physical skills. Physical skills will be taught throughout this series of lessons on self-defense.

Key Points to Remember

1. Self-defense skills are survival skills
2. Self-defense begins with self-esteem
3. The three levels of defense are:
   Prevention
   Psychological
   Physical

LESSON TWO
Physical Defense—Basic Skills: The Stance and the Punch

The Fighting Stance

You assume the fighting stance whenever you get prepared to fight. This may be well in advance, or it may be after someone has attacked you. A stance serves both psychological and physical purposes.

Psychologically, the stance sends out the message that you are prepared: you know what you are doing; you are able to defend yourself; and in essence, no one had better *mess with you.*

Physically, the stance is the position from which you fight. In this position, you are at a right angle to the assailant, and your vital areas are protected. Your arms are in a protective position, and your fists and feet are ready to attack, if necessary. Since much of your power comes from your legs—and your legs must be bent in order to maximize this force—the stance is a power position. By crouching down, you have more stability and balance; yet, because of the nature of the position, you are able to quickly move backward or forward as need be. By being in the stance, you are able to maneuver, yet still make eye contact with your opponent. Therefore, the stance is the ideal fighting position.

Here is How to Get Into the Stance:

1. Stand with your left side (if you are right-handed) to the assailant. This will present the smallest target to the person you are fighting.

2. Place your legs a comfortable distance apart (one to two feet,) pointing your left foot at the assailant.

3. Bend your arms at the elbows, holding them a little away from your body.

4. Clench your fist

Making the fist

1. Curl your thumbs on the outside of your fists so that they are outside and on top of your first two fingers.

2. In punching, concentrate your force on the upper knuckles of these two fingers.

3. Keep your wrist tight and straight. Without a tight fist, your blows will be weak and you may injure your wrist or hand (Figure 5.)

The basic fighting stance:

FIGURE 3. Front view   FIGURE 4. Side view

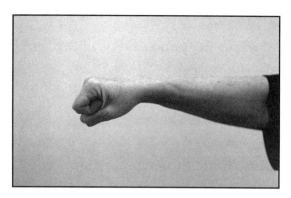

FIGURE 5. The clenched fist

Adjusting Your Distance

Whether you are attacking or defending, you need to adjust your distance according to whether you want to make contact with your blows or evade the assailant's blows. When you attack (or counterattack) you may have to move toward the assailant, since he may be out of range, or your attack may be aggressively pushing him back.

To move forward

From your stance, step with your front foot first, then your rear foot. Take small, quick, even steps. Keep your torso erect. If the assailant attacks you with a punch, shove or kick, move out of range.

To move backward

From your stance step back with your back foot first, then your front foot.

Sidestepping is used when an assailant attacks you with a knife or broken bottle and will be discussed in the section on weapons defense.

The Punch

The clenched-fist punch is one of the very first skills to master because, as you learn to punch, you learn how to utilize force and power—principles that must be employed in every attack or defense.

Arm Coordination

1. Start with the basic fighting stance.
2. Clench your fists.
3. Wind-up by bringing your right elbow straight back, palm up, so that your upper arm is parallel to the floor.

Delivering the Punch

1. First, wind up for the punch (See Figure 6). You will now do four things at the same time:
2. Raise your rear heel and pivot counterclockwise on the ball of this foot, thrusting down and back so that you practically straighten your rear leg (See Figure 7).
3. Swing your right hip forward, squaring off your shoulders. Keep your left knee bent and your torso erect. Do not lean forward. Your weight remains evenly distributed on both legs
4. Yell
5. Attack by punching decisively
6. You aim your attack at the assailant's Adam's apple. Thrust your arm forward so that, upon impact, it is palm down. The front arm acts in opposition to the rear arm. At the same time the rear arm thrusts forward, the front arm moves back to the side, bent at the elbow, palm up. Your arms are then ready for the second punch.

The Second Punch

To punch a second time, immediately wind up the left arm, and, without losing momentum, punch as fast and as forcefully as possible. Do not move your feet. They remain in

 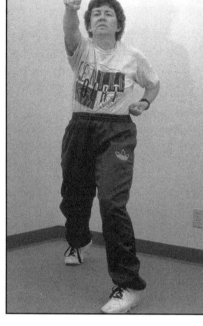

FIGURE 6. The punch: wind-up   FIGURE 7. The punch: delivery

the forward thrust position that you have just completed in the first punch. Make sure you yell twice. In order to increase the speed of your second punch, increase the speed of your yell. It really works!

Yelling As A Weapon

You have to yell!!! When you chose to take these lessons, you chose to learn how to fight. Whether or not you like to yell depends on your background and personality. It doesn't matter whether you like to yell or want to yell. *You have to yell!!!* Why? After all, if you yell and make a loud noisy scene, people may watch. Perhaps you have been taught that it's polite to be silent. That is exactly what the assailant wants and counts on. I will tell you exactly why you must yell.

Research finds that yelling is one of the most effective resistance strategies. (Chapter 4 of *Exploding the Myth of Self-Defense* describes the research conducted on rape avoidance and resistance.) A physical defense or attack cannot be effectively executed without yelling. Yelling startles and intimidates the assailant, and yelling increases your physical power by bringing more oxygen to your muscles and stimulating the flow of adrenaline.

Reach deep into your inner self, breathe from your diagram—as if you were singing in a chorus—and belt out a loud blood curdling battle cry! (We will discuss more on this battle cry in LESSON THREE—How to Win—The Psychology of Fighting Back.)

How To Practice Physical Skills

Whether you practice with a male or a female is a matter of personal preference. The attitude of your practice partner, however, must be supportive of your efforts. If you practice with a female friend who doesn't take you seriously or who discounts your intent to learn, or if you practice with a male friend whose ego gets in the way, you are preparing yourself to lose. Some students have told me that in practicing with their boyfriends they were unsuccessful in thwarting attacks. If this were to continue, the student would begin to doubt the effectiveness of the techniques learned in class. In one such case, I asked the individual if she was really angry at her friend during practice and if she was willing to incapacitate him during the session. The young woman replied, "Of course not!"

Sometimes, the only way to break out of a hold is to force the attacker to let go by incapacitating him. In real situations, your anger and outrage will add higher levels of adrenaline to your blood, giving you greater strength. Both anger and outrage were absent from the home practice session described above.

It is important in setting up a practice session to have some rules to practice by. Practice only with a supportive partner. Make an agreement that your partner will release his or her hold or stop the attack if you simulate a counterattack that is incapacitating. Your partner should agree not to release her or his hold too easily; otherwise you will develop a false sense of what will and will not work. First work slowly at a new skill to make sure you have perfected the mechanics. Once this is done, increase your speed. Then, incorporate aggressive body and verbal language into the session.

FIGURE 8. Using an armshield for practice

Practice Drills

By Yourself

The stance
Stand in front of a mirror. Get into a stance. Clench your fists. Check your position. Is your weight balanced on both feet? Is your side facing the mirror? Are your knees bent and thighs pushed out? Do you look like you know what you are doing?

The punch
Check your punch. Is your back leg practically straightened? Did you pivot on the ball of your back foot? Is the position of your fist rotated down in the front and up in the back? Do you feel balanced?

The second punch
Punch twice. Check to see that you don't rotate your back foot on the second punch. Did you yell twice?

With a Partner
1. Practice moving and distance. Stand in opposition to each other and get into the stance position. One person moves, either forward or backward, and the other person moves in response. Make sure to stay an even distance apart.

2. Practice with either a pillow or an armshield. When you hold the armshield, be in the stance power position (as if you had just completed a punch) so that you are firmly braced. Hold the armshield out in front of you at the height of the Adam's apple. Your partner first punches in slow motion, then faster with force and power, yelling as she punches.

LESSON THREE
How To Win—The Psychology of Fighting Back

Victimization and Personal Power

Blaming the Victim

If you have ever been the victim of assault, rape, incest, abuse, harassment, battering, or anything else, it is extremely important for you to not blame yourself. The society that we live in is very good at pointing the finger of blame at the victim of a crime, rather than at the criminal. For example, if a woman is raped and she didn't fiercely fight in an attempt to prevent the rape, many times she is blamed for the rape. Does this make any sense? If you understand the psychology of intimidation, as we will discuss later in this lesson, you will understand why she didn't fight. If a young woman is raped by her date in her own home, she frequently is blamed because it is assumed that she must have lead him on.

If you have ever been the victim of a crime, you did whatever you could, under the circumstances, to survive. By reading this book or taking a class in self-defense, you are taking a very positive step in helping yourself and in regaining your personal power.

People become victims because they don't know that they have any other options. Since self-defense skills are survival skills, you learn new techniques for surviving in a crisis situation. You learn what works, what doesn't work, and why. The definition of personal power is that you have control. You know your options and make your own choices. You are resolved that no one will ever take your power away from you again.

Learning to Win

I play tennis. Several years ago, I took up this sport both for my health and for my enjoyment. I have been playing competitive tennis for about a year. When I first started competing, I lost every match. I can tell you that this is no fun. Then I joined a team and improved my skills. I started to win some matches, but I still lost matches. I learned the reason why. I lost matches because I really didn't know how to win. I discussed how to win with different people—to no avail. But then one day, I was asked to play a match against the best player in the league. She had beaten our best player several months before. It was in this match that I learned how to win. Tennis matches usually last about an hour and a half or two hours at the most. This match lasted for four hours! I was determined. After the first set of games, I developed a blister on my left little toe. After the second set, I developed a blister on my right little toe. I could hardly walk. It was agony to retrieve the balls. I continued to play. Around the third hour, my opponent stated that the one who would win the match was the one that was the most determined. I won the match! And by winning, I learned the secret of how to win. You win with pure guts and determination.

This lesson is true for self-defense as well. You win because you are determined to win. You expect nothing less, and you will accept nothing less. *Winning is an attitude. Winning is having no other options in your mind. Winning is pure guts and determination.*

Developing Your Intuition

Developing your sixth sense and listening to it is one of the most important self-defense skills that you can learn. The benefits of doing this are immeasurable. If you sense that something is wrong, it is. If an alarm sounds in the pit of your stomach—a gut feeling—that you sense that something is not exactly right, then something is not exactly right. The alarm that goes off does not have to be loud. The fact that a vague alarm was sounded is more than enough for you to act.

Denial

Why do people hesitate and not immediately act, or why do they not act at all? I believe that one major reason for this is denial. Betty, a former student of mine, reported that she went to an automatic teller machine (ATM) late one Sunday night. The ATM was located in a deserted suburban shopping center. As she approached the ATM, Betty sensed that something was wrong. She looked up and noticed that a man was standing approximately ten feet away from her. He was holding an orange garbage bag, and looking straight at her. This did not compute. Something was wrong. Betty did not want anything to be wrong. She thought that maybe the man was with the janitorial service. She then thought that maybe he was waiting for the ATM. If so, why was he staring at her? Although Betty felt uneasy, she did nothing about it. Then the man started coming up to her, and the alarm went off loud and clear! Betty got into her fighting stance, whipped out a canister of tear gas, yelled, and shot the man in the face with it. He screamed, dropped down, and she ran away. Betty was fortunate. She did the right thing—albeit a little bit late. She found out later that this man was the "orange garbage bag rapist"—a criminal who had been stalking this particular shopping center for weeks.

As you develop your power and your ability to recognize your intuitive warnings, you will be better able to act on them. This skill is so important because not only will it keep you from harm's way, but it will help you ferret out those areas in your life that are not consistent with your new sense of personal power and control.

Understanding Assault Patterns

The basic assault pattern, which transcends just about every type of attack is target, test, and attack. I have found this pattern to be true no matter what the type of attack. This ranges from stranger rape on the street to acquaintance rape in someone's home, to sexual harassment in the office. (For a complete discussion of the cause, prevention, and methods of dealing with sexual harassment, read *Exploding The Myth of Self-Defense*, Chapter Seven—Sexual Harassment.)

Target

Criminals want to be successful. Why would it make sense for them to pick on someone who is likely to beat them up. They target the weakest, most vulnerable victims that they can find. That is why they attack people who are disabled, seniors, children, and women. They do not think that people in these categories will be able to offer much resistance.

Criminals often target people because of location. The location of choice is one which is termed "isolated." This could mean a deserted street, or it could mean your own home if a hostile individual is inside and wishes to hurt you.

The third, and in my opinion, the most important factor in targeting, is that assailants choose potential victims who are not prepared psychologically to fight back. When I speak to someone who has been assaulted in public, I ask this person a simple question. "Where did the assailant come from?" The answer is usually the same, "Nowhere" or "I don't know." This proves to me that the person who was victimized was not paying attention. People also may not be psychologically prepared if they are intoxicated, talking to friends, lost, depressed, or thinking of other things.

Test

Once the assailant has targeted his potential victim, he must perform one other step before attacking. This is the intimidation test. Intimidation can take many forms. It can be verbal or non-verbal body language. It could be physical. He might put his arm on you or grab you. The assailant may threaten to harm you if you do not do what he says. He may even hit you.

Attack

If you flunk the intimidation test, he will attack.

Countering Assault Patterns

With the knowledge of assailants' target —test—attack patterns, we can first learn how to prevent targeting from taking place in the first place and learn how to break the pattern, if necessary.

Radar

Don't get targeted in the first place. Is this easy to say and hard to do? Absolutely not. Traditional thinking and advice will tell you not to go anywhere or do anything which might put you in harm's way. For example, if you are female, you are warned not to jog by yourself. If you are a senior, you are counseled not to go out after dark. And certainly, don't travel by yourself. The message rings loud and clear. You cannot take care of yourself. Traditional thinking and advice will not only keep you out of harm's way, it will keep you powerless and in a box of fear.

You cannot change who you are. Many times you cannot or do not choose to change your location. Does this mean that you are subject to be targeted, even if you are in a high risk group? No. There is something that you can change. When you make this change, everything else changes too. What you change is your attitude!

Times have changed. It used to be that you could walk down the street and, under most sets of circumstances, hardly need to pay attention. When I was a child in New York City, it was common practice for mothers to park their children's strollers in front of the department store and go inside to shop. Today, you wouldn't leave the stroller for fear that it would be stolen. Back then, mothers would leave their children in the stroller, with no fear that the child would be gone when they came back. The only time I had a problem with that as a child was one day when my mother forgot me (to my older sister's delight). She walked one block away and then suddenly remembered I was still parked outside the department store.

Today, you need to be constantly aware when you are out in public. That is your job. When you are out with your friends, you still need to be aware. I have had too many stories reported to me of people attacked in public when they were chatting with their friends.

Although you are aware, it doesn't mean that you are tense. When you are powerful, your body language exudes confidence. When you are both powerful and aware, your body language sends out the signal that you know where you are going, that you know what you are doing, that you are confident and alert, and that you respect yourself. When you do this, you rarely get targeted. Only if you are aware, can you recognize your gut warning feelings that something is wrong.

Don't Mess With Me

If you consider the situation dangerous, or if you sense that something is wrong, then it is time to go to the next level of awareness— *Don't mess with me! Don't mess with me!* is an attitude. It is a signal to all potential assailants to keep away from you. Diane, a 98 pound, 4'11" woman, who tells her story in *Exploding The Myth of Self-Defense* describes the *Don't mess with me!* signal very eloquently. You would think that she, being a small women, would be a target. Not Diane! She is a master of *street smarts*. Although she lives in a major city, Diane easily traverses even the worse areas of this city. Here is her secret.

"Wherever I go in the city, I go with a purpose. I don't fear being accosted by anyone. My pace is often fast. I am alert; I am aware of where I am. I know where I am going. People don't bother me. ...I don't stop and converse with anyone. Even when people try to talk to me I give them a smile and keep going. I've never been disrespected by anyone on the streets. I am constantly looking around and behind me no matter where I am. Sometimes I am so tired that my face says 'don't bother me.' I am the worst person to deal with when I am tired, so 'stay out of my face!' I have that look that also slays 'bother me and you are dead meat!' I face people and situations. I watch people and keep going wherever it is I am going. ...My back is straight and my stride is that of a confident person. ...I stand at the bus stops without worrying about anyone bothering me, and it is the same when I am on the buses. I can sit in the back on the worst bus routes and show no fear. Why walk in fear? But whenever a situation may arise in which I would need to react, I will act with confidence.

"I don't like threats. So far this has not happened to me either. I don't take them kindly. No one has the right to try to take my confidence in myself away. I won't allow that. I have too many things to do and places to go. Why let someone take myself away from myself? I am important to me. I simply will not allow my space and peace of mind to be violated."

If, despite all your preventive measures, an attack is imminent, then you need to go to the next step, raging.

Raging

If I were only allowed one piece of advice—the one thing that would say it all, in terms of fighting back—it would be raging. This is the secret of self-defense! Take all the anger that you have built up in your entire lifetime, and blast it at the assailant! The results are remarkable. In fact, the results are so remarkable, that raging is the major ingredient in every single success story that has come back to me in the 21 years that I have been teaching self-defense! Here is an example.

Some years ago, my partner and I were driving though a dangerous part of the city. Our new car's radiator overheated. We pulled over to the curb. While I was pouring water into the radiator a man approached my partner. He invaded her personal space, towered over her and threatened her with a pipe wrench. She was so angry that her new car had broken down and was furious that someone would want to hurt us. She turned into a force field of fury and raged at him. The man dropped his wrench and tripped over the curb as he ran away!

Transformations

Lori, a woman who has taken my self-defense class, told me this story. "I came home from work. I was still outside on the pathway to my home when I noticed that a man was picking the lock on my back door. My two children were inside. I became very angry because he was violating my home and threatening my children. I started shouting at him. I was furious. (Prior to my taking the self-defense class I would have been frozen in my tracks—unable to do anything.) He looked up at me and was completely startled. He started making excuses—that he was looking for someone else. I shouted that that person didn't live there—that he didn't belong there. Then, an amazing thing happened. I transformed. The transformation was triggered by the fury. I pushed my hands out at him and felt really powerful. I visualized that my hands and body were getting larger and larger. I must have psychically overpowered him because he fell off the porch (which was four feet high) and ran away."

In my classes, I ask my students to think about what they would like to become when they fight back. Common responses are:

- a raging bear
- a volcano erupting
- a black panther who is ready to strike
- a cobra ready to strike
- a roaring wave
- a tigress protecting her cubs
- a mountain lion about to pounce
- a wolf bearing her teeth
- an angry gorilla

Think of who you would become. Visualize it. Picture very clearly the size of this creature, its shape, its color, its battle cry. Give it a name. Then practice becoming your transformed self.

Responding to the Fears of Fighting

In LESSON ONE, we discussed the common fears that women express that might prevent an effective defense. It is time to expose and remove them.

"I am afraid that I will freeze—that I will try to scream and that nothing will come out."

This is the most common of all the fears. In fact, many women have nightmares of being attacked and yelling soundlessly. The way not to panic in a crisis situation is through training. You become prepared by knowing your options and which one has the greatest chance of working. Knowledge and practice, as well as the belief in your ability to respond appropriately in a crisis situation, will dispel this fear.

"I am afraid that I will hit him but won't hurt him."

Knowledge, training, and practice will allay this fear. When you learn how to strike the vulnerable areas of the body and learn how easy it is to incapacitate someone, the fear will be gone.

"I am afraid of big men because I am small."

Size has nothing to do with your ability to effectively fight back and win. The limiting factor is purely psychological. Assaultive men commonly use their larger size to intimidate women or smaller men or children. Everyone, regardless of size, has the same vulnerable areas. Your job is to psychologically take him off guard and attack his target areas. Since he cannot physically strengthen his vulnerable areas, even a woman who is five feet tall will have no problem striking the Adam's apple of a man who is six feet tall.

"I am afraid to get him angry."

The assailant really ought to fear angering you! It really doesn't matter how angry he gets because when you incapacitate him, he cannot hurt you.

"I am afraid that if I try to fight back I will get killed."

If you don't fight back, you will be in the assailant's control, and he can do anything that he wants to you.

"I am afraid to fight because I might get hurt."

This fear arises out of a lack of experience in contact physical activities (such as contact team sports—football, wrestling, the martial arts). Boys learn from childhood that if they get hit, they will not fall apart. If you have ever played in a competitive sport, you do not usually feel getting shoved, or getting hit with the ball. You only become aware of it the next day when you notice a black and blue mark and wonder where it came from.

"I am afraid to hurt anyone."

Female conditioning is to not hurt anyone. Each of us must live with our own code of ethics. I strongly believe that people need to respect the rights of others. However, when someone tries to violate your rights as a human being or when someone tries to take away your integrity, then all rules are off! It is your legal and moral right to do whatever you need to do in self-defense to preserve your integrity as a human being. You need to take care of yourself. You incapacitate an assailant so that he cannot hurt you.

"I am afraid that I will get too angry and lose control."

You won't. When you are trained in both physical and psychological self-defense, you will be in control of the situation. You will know exactly what is occurring. You will therefore be able to choose your options and successfully fight and win!

Key Points to Remember

1. The definition of personal power is that you have control. You know your options and make your own choices. You are resolved that no one will ever take your power away from you.

2. Learn to win. *Winning is an attitude. Winning is having no other options in your mind. Winning is pure guts and determination.*

3. Developing your intuition and listening to it is one of the most important self-defense skills that you can learn.

4. Assault patterns encompass targeting, testing, and attacking.

5. Raging is the single most important piece of advice in fighting back and winning.

LESSON FOUR
Physical Defense—Basic Skills: Kicking

Colleen is a young woman who is a survivor of acquaintance rape and is a past student in my self-defense class. She was making a call at a phone booth when several men came up and tried to assault her. She got angry, yelled, *leave me alone,* sent out bad vibes, and kicked at them. She broke one man's kneecap and the other two dragged him off. Sound good? That would have been good for anyone. One thing was different here. Colleen is blind!

Kicking may be your best attack, for several reasons—especially the psychological tactic of surprise. Kicking is just not expected, especially by women. A second reason for kicking is force. Because your legs are stronger that your arms, you can kick harder than you can punch. A third reason is that your legs are longer than your assailant's arms, so you can kick him from beyond the range of his arms. Fourth, if you kick low (aiming in most cases at the kneecap), your kick is hard to block, and very effective in incapacitating the assailant. It is for all these reasons that I recommend kicking whenever possible.

The Front Snap Kick

1. Start from the stance. (If you don't have time to assume your stance before you kick or if it would ruin the element of surprise, get into the stance as you kick.)

Figure 9. (Left)
The front snap kick: raising the knee

Figure 10. (Left below)
The front snap kick: snapping
the foot straight

Figure 11. (Right below)
The front snap kick:
retracting the foot

2. Using your back leg, raise your leg so that your thigh is parallel to the ground, as shown in Figure 9. (This will work for most assailants, since kneecaps are almost at the same level for adults—even someone who is six feet tall vs. someone who is five feet tall.)

3. At the same time as you are lifting your back leg, flex your ankle upward and curl your toes upward.

4. Snap the foot straight forward, aiming through the assailant's kneecap and making contact with the ball of your foot (Figure 10).

5. Immediately retract your foot so it cannot be grabbed, and then bring your foot down into the stance (Figure 11). Whether you bring your leg forward or backward into the stance will depend upon your adjustment for distance, which we discussed in Lesson Two.

6. If you have trouble balancing, lean forward slightly and bend at the waist.

7. Your kick needs to be made forcefully and quickly, in continuous motion, without hesitation and without telegraphing your attack. (This means that you keep your eyes riveted on the assailant's eyes.) Be sure to yell!

The Side Kick

This kick is used when you want to attack someone positioned at your side, or someone in front of you who is a little further away than you can reach with the snap kick. When you employ the side kick, use the leg that is closest to the assailant.

1. To kick with your right leg, put your weight on your left foot, drop your left shoulder, and lift your right knee. The height to which you raise your knee depends upon the height of the target you are kicking (Figure 12).

2. Kick to the side, making contact with the flat part of your foot. Depending upon the position of the assailant, your side kick should be aimed at his kneecap or at the side of his knee (Figure 13).

3. Immediately retract your leg and return to the starting position (Figure 14).

Figure 12.
The side kick:
launching the kick

Figure 13.
The side kick:
aimed at the
assailant's kneecap

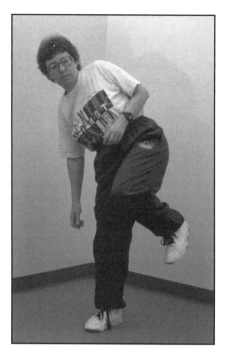

Figure 14.
The side kick:
retracting the leg

The Side Kick—Kicking to the Front

First pivot so that your side is to the assailant, then kick.

The Back Kick

This kick is similar to the side kick. Pivot so that your side is to the assailant, then kick as you would in a side kick (Figure 15).

Figure 15.
The back kick

Practice Drills

By Yourself

Stand in front of a mirror and go through each of the kicking instructions. First kick in slow motion, then increase your speed. Notice the difference when you kick in silence, and when you let out a bloodcurdling battle cry!

With a Partner

Use a pillow or armshield. Kneel or squat down and hold the armshield kneecap distance high, away from your own knee. First kick in slow motion, then increase speed and power. Yell!!!

LESSON FIVE
How to Fight and Win

What You Need to Know About the Laws of Self-Defense

Each of us has the legal and moral right to defend ourselves. Although laws of self-defense are fairly similar, I suggest checking your local laws so that you know exactly what is legal and what is not where you live.

The law of self-defense states that if someone physically attacks you, you have the right to fight back, using whatever force is reasonable and necessary to prevent injury to yourself. You can meet force with force, but the force must not be excessive to the perceived danger.

You can also fight back (or attack first) if you believe that bodily injury is about to be inflicted. In this case, four elements need to be present.

- *Threat*

Someone is threatening you with attack. The threat can be verbal, non-verbal or both.

- *Intent*

You as a reasonable person, must believe that the assailant intends to attack you. This means that if someone else were in your shoes, they would believe that the same thing was about to happen to them.

- *Ability*

The attacker must have the physical ability to attack you.

- *Opportunity*

The assailant must have the physical opportunity to attack you. If, for example, his back was turned, he might not be considered to have the opportunity.

If all these elements are present, you can fight back first, before the assailant actually ever touches you. As in the physical attack described above, you have the right to fight back, using whatever force is reasonable and necessary to prevent injury to yourself.

How can you tell if all the above elements are present? The best way I know of is to trust your intuition—your gut feeling. If someone is threatening you, and you have that unmistakable feeling in the pit of your stomach, I suggest fighting back.

Self-defense must be immediate. Once the immediate danger has passed, it is not self-defense to go after the other person and attack him.

Self-defense is considered the defense of self, or the defense of another individual. It is not considered self-defense to protect property, unless you feel that you are in danger of being attacked.

Principles of Fighting

You will be most successful if you incorporate effective fighting principles. These principles are interrelated and need to be coordinated with each other, as needed. They are relatively simple skills that can be learned in a short time.

Once learned, however, they must be practiced regularly until they become second nature. Fighting back effectively is a learned and trained response.

1. Fight to Win

When you make the decision to fight back, do so with the full commitment to win. Anything less diminishes your effectiveness. If you think you are going to lose, you probably will. You must not make a halfhearted attempt to fight back. *Winning is an attitude. Winning is having no other options in your mind. Winning is pure guts and determination.*

2. Resist Immediately

An assailant does not expect you to fight back. Otherwise, you would not have been targeted in the first place. The assailant expects a passive, frightened, submissive victim. In most cases, the key to successful fighting is forceful, immediate resistance. By doing this, you surprise the attacker, and take advantage of his disorientation by quickly incapacitating him.

3. Yell Loudly

As mentioned in LESSON TWO, yelling is an important weapon. It is used as both physical and a psychological weapon. Since we all are afraid of loud, unexpected sounds, the yell will disorient an assailant and, in addition, possibly attract attention. Yelling will also help you physically and psychologically to be more aggressive. It opens your breathing and brings more oxygen to your brain and your muscles. Therefore, you will be more powerful and project an aura of fury. Make sure that your yell is a loud, vicious battle cry that rises from your diaphragm and is directed at the assailant.

Take a deep breath, open your mouth, look mean and vicious, and yell. Do this every single time you punch, kick, block, break from a hold, and counterattack.

4. Maintain Eye Contact

Look directly into the assailant's eyes in order to intimidate him. In addition, the eye contact will prevent you from looking at the area you are about to strike, which telegraphs your moves.

5. Start Raging

When you are fighting or confronting the assailant, you must send out a force field of fury (See LESSON TWO). Your body language tells the attacker unequivocally that you mean business. You are communicating to him (with your eyes, your voice, and your body language) that you are angry, outraged, furious. Look directly into his eyes, with an intimidating *drop dead* glare; snarl, flare your nostrils, and move toward him, pushing him back. Direct toward him all the anger that has been building inside of you during your entire lifetime. He will quickly get the message that he picked the wrong person to attack and that he had better try to leave as fast as he can. The typical response to your force field of fury will be to almost blow the assailant away. In many cases, he will be gone even before you have a chance to physically attack him.

6. Fight From the Stance Position

Immediately assume the fighting stance position when you start to fight back. A correct stance may ward off an attack, and a correct stance will enable you to launch an effective attack or defense.

7. Target Your Attack

It doesn't matter how big or strong the assailant is. He will be seriously disabled if attacked in vulnerable areas. Therefore, these areas are your target. It does you more harm than good to hurt the attacker. For example, if you kick him in the shin, it takes time, does not stop him, and loses you the element of surprise. Kicking him in the kneecap does stop him. Attacking target areas will be discussed in LESSON SIX.

Key Points to Remember

1. The law of self-defense states that if someone physically attacks you, you have the right to fight back, using whatever force is reasonable and necessary to prevent injury to yourself.

2. Learn and practice your fundamental fighting skills and principles until they become automatic. You can then be free to concentrate on dealing with the situation rather than worrying about your body position.

3. Fight to Win!

LESSON SIX
Physical Defense—Basic Skills: Blocking and Counterattacking

Blocking

Blocking is crucial to your defense. It is a means of deflecting an attack to prevent it from reaching you. The principles of blocking are as follows:

1. Move Back on the Block

If someone is attacking you, it is best for you to move away from the direction of the attack. Moving back will (a) lesson the impact of the attack, (b) possibly throw the assailant off balance, and (c) give you more time to respond to the attack.

2. Use Full Force in Executing a Block

You need maximum power to divert a forceful attack. To maximize power, wind up, take your stance, clench your fists, and block quickly.

3. Block Away from Your Body, not Toward It

Aim the direction of your block away from your body area. If the attack is aimed at or toward your right side, block with your right arm; if the attack is aimed at or toward your left side, block with your left arm. Suppose, for example, the attacker has a broken bottle and swings it across you body in the direction of your left shoulder. If you use your right arm to block, rather than your left, you will bring the bottle across your face.

4. Block to Protect a Specific Zone

In most ball games you strike a specific object (a ball); when you block, however, you protect a specific area of your body. If you bat at the attacker's arm, you protect only a small area, perhaps only as wide as your fist. Consequently, you must block to protect an entire zone without attempting to strike directly at the assailant's arm. In so doing, you will cover a greater area, and the assailant's arm will be deflected so that it does not reach you.

5. Stop the Block Just Beyond Your Body Area

It is counterproductive to follow through on the block. Swinging your arm out of line will carry you off balance and prevent you from making an immediate counterattack. Be sure, however, to complete the block by going through the full range of motion, and by not stopping short.

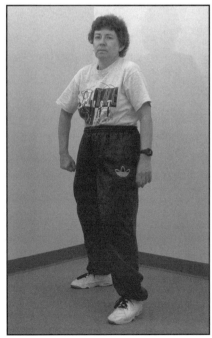

FIGURE 16. (left page to left) The downward block: the wind-up

FIGURE 17. (left page to right) The downward block: the block

FIGURE 18. The downward block: correct arm position

The Downward Block

This block is used to deflect attacks directed toward your lower body. Use either your right or left arm, depending upon the direction of the attack.

1. From your stance, with your fist clenched, wind up by placing your arm upward across your body with your fist facing and almost touching the opposite shoulder (Figure 16.)

2. Forcefully swing your arm diagonally downward—yelling as you do so—crossing your body, stopping directly next to the outside of the thigh, fist facing inward. The elbow remains slightly bent, and the distance between the fist and the thigh is about six inches (Figure 17).

3. Make contact with the assailant's arm, between his elbow and wrist (Figure 18).

4. Move back as you block. To do this, step back with your back foot first, then your front foot. Take small, quick steps.

The Upward Block

This block is used to deflect an attack aimed at your waist or above.

1. Wind up by placing your arm downward across your body, fist clenched, palm facing inward, so that your fist is opposite your hip, as if you were going to draw a sword out of its sheath (Figure 19).

2. With your elbow bent, swing your arm diagonally upward and outward across your body. The arc of this swing passes across your nose and stops directly opposite the temple Figure 20). Your palm will be facing inward, your upper arm parallel to the floor, and your forearm perpendicular to the floor. (The elbow will be at a right angle, and you will be in a "making a muscle" position.) Make contact with the assailant's arm between his elbow and wrist (Figure 21).

FIGURE 19.
The upward block:
wind-up

FIGURE 20. (left)
The upward block: the block

FIGURE 21. (right)
The upward block:
correct arm position

Counterattacking

The way to respond to an attack is to prevent it from reaching you, as we discussed above. The second step, then, is to counterattack with multiple blows, kicks, or gouges aimed at vulnerable target areas. Sometimes you may have to attack first, as when a person threatens you and you believe that an assault is imminent.

Adjust Your Distance

Whether you are attacking or defending, you need to adjust your distance according to whether you want to make contact with your blows or evade the assailant's blows. When you attack or counterattack, move toward the assailant. This is done because he may have moved out of range, and/or your attack is aggressively pushing him back.

If the assailant attacks you, move out of range. You move back from a punch, kick or shove, and sidestep if the attack is with a knife or similar weapon. Sidestepping will be discussed in the section on weapons defense.

Target Your Attack

As discussed on Page 55, you target your attacks. You attack one or more of these areas in rapid succession, in combination with other psychological and physical attacks, and keep attacking until you have incapacitated the assailant. Your target depends on three things: (1) the area you can reach; (2) the area that is left exposed; (3) your distance from the assailant. In this section, we will discuss specific ways of attacking target areas.

Target areas are shown in Figure 22. The body has many vital spots; of these it is best to concentrate on several that you can strike quickly in succession and that are easily accessible. Aim your attacks through the following target areas: eyes, neck, nose, groin, knee.

The Eyes

As the most vulnerable area of the body, eyes can be gouged, causing temporary or permanent blindness and excruciating pain. Don't be squeamish about attacking the eyes. In a crisis situation, this technique may save your life.

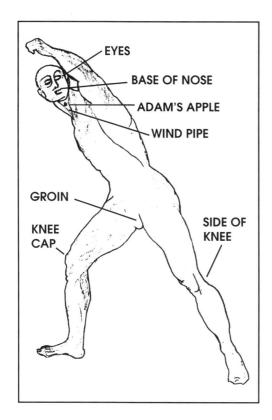

FIGURE 22. Target Areas

EYES
BASE OF NOSE
ADAM'S APPLE
WIND PIPE
GROIN
KNEE CAP
SIDE OF KNEE

The thumb gouge

Grasp the sides of the attacker's head with both hands, fingers spread apart. Firmly hold his head with your fingers and forcefully thrust your thumbs into the eyes (Figure 23).

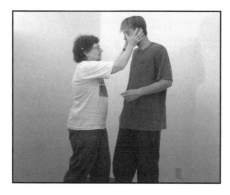

FIGURE 23. The thumb gouge

The finger jab to eyes

Spread your fingers apart and keep your fingers and wrist rigid. Using full force, jab with all four fingers into the eyes (Figure 24). If the assailant is wearing glasses, aim just under the rim of the glasses and continue up into the eyes.

The Neck

Blows to the neck can cause excruciating pain, unconsciousness, and severe injury.

Punch to the Adam's apple

The Adam's apple is an easy target because in men it projects outward. Use a clenched-fist punch (Figure 25) or an elbow smash (Figure 26). To execute an elbow smash, clench your fist and bring your arm up to chest level. Using your other hand to hold your fist will strengthen the thrust of the attack. Keep your elbow bent and thrust it into the assailant's Adam's apple.

FIGURE 24.
Finger jab to eyes

FIGURE 25.
Punch to the Adam's apple

FIGURE 26.
Elbow smash to Adam's apple

Blow to the windpipe

In order to get maximum force into this relatively small hollow area, attack the windpipe with an extended knuckle blow. The mechanics of punching are the same as in the clenched-fist punch. To extend your knuckles, first make a clenched fist. Then keeping the first two fingers together, extend their knuckles outward (Figure 27).

FIGURE 27.
Blow to the windpipe

Blow to the back of neck

The back of the neck is usually attacked as a secondary area in combination with another attack. For example, after you have kneed the attacker in the groin, he may double over, exposing the back of his neck. You can attack this area with a blow, striking this area with the side of your arm (Figure 28).

FIGURE 28.
Blow to back of neck

The Nose

The nose is a sensitive area that bleeds readily. Strikes to the nose are painful and can cause unconsciousness.

Strike to the base of the nose

Strike the base of the nose with the heel of your hand, with your force directed back and upward. Flex your wrist back slightly and use the same force as if you were punching (Figure 29).

FIGURE 29.
Strike to the base
of the nose

The Groin

The groin is a highly vulnerable area in males. A forceful hit to the groin causes excruciating pain and unconsciousness and can thus immobilize the attacker. Caution: Because the assailant may expect a hit to the groin and be prepared for it, your attack to this area must be a complete surprise.

Knee to groin

This is a close-range attack. Lift your knee forcefully under the groin as if you were going to execute a snap kick (Figure 30).

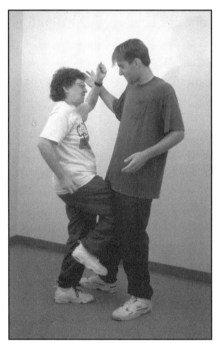

FIGURE 30. Knee to groin

Groin pull

Reach your hand between the assailant's legs, grab his testicles, squeeze, and pull.

The Knee

The knee is highly vulnerable, and even forty pounds of force directed at the knee cap will cause enough damage to immobilize the attacker.

Snap kick to knee

If the assailant is in front of you, execute a snap kick to his kneecap (Refer to Figure 10).

If you are not already in your stance, assume your stance as you kick, otherwise, you will telegraph your attack.

Side kick to knee

If the assailant is at your side, execute a side kick to the knee (Refer to Figure 13).

Back kick to knee

If the assailant has grabbed you from behind, kick his kneecap with a back kick (Refer to Figure 15).

Practice Drills

By Yourself

Stand in front of a mirror and go through each of the blocking instructions. First block in slow motion, then increase your speed.

After you have mastered the blocks, combine them with punches and kicks aimed at vulnerable areas.

Drill 1

Step back and block.

Drill 2

Step back and block. Counterattack by punching twice.

Drill 3

Step back and block. Step forward and punch twice.

Drill 4

Step back and block. Kick, using a snap kick, recover forward in your stance.

Drill 5

Step back and block. Kick, using a snap kick, recover forward in your stance. Punch twice.

With a Partner

Use a pillow or armshield. Practice blocking and counterattacking.

LESSON SEVEN
Rape and Sexual Assault Prevention—Stranger Attacks

In LESSON THREE: How To Win—The Psychology of Fighting Back, we discussed the assault patterns of target/test/attack and how to counter these patterns. Now let us deal specifically with the issue of rape avoidance and resistance strategies.

Sexual assault is committed by someone you don't know, or someone you know. Stranger rape refers to an assault by someone whom you do not know. Acquaintance rape refers to an assault by someone you do know, either casually or intimately. When the rapist is someone you are dating, the attack is referred to as date rape. When the rapist is your spouse, the attack is referred to as spousal rape.

There is an extensive body of research on the subject of rape resistance. Chapters Four and Five of *Exploding The Myth of Self-Defense—A Survival Guide for Every Woman* analyze and discuss just about all the published research on rape avoidance and defense. In this lesson, I am going to summarize what the research tells us: fight back, fight back, fight back!

Strategies for Countering Stranger Attacks

Traditional advice is conflicting advice. Suppose you were told that if you fight back you will probably get hurt. Would you fight? Perhaps it would be better to talk to the rapist and convince him that you are a human being? Isn't this non-violent approach safer? Maybe if you do nothing, someonemay come by and rescue you. Why not plead and beg? You could even cry. If none of this works, you might try cooperation. After all, we have been taught that it is rude to make a scene in public. Nice people are cooperative, understanding, and do not fight. All this advice will do is to get you raped.

We need to address and have answers to the following questions:

• What strategies are effective?

• What strategies are ineffective or even harmful?

• What strategies are effective if the assailant has a weapon?

• Do individuals who physically resist suffer injury?

All the studies that I have reviewed say the same thing. The research tells you what doesn't work and what works.

The following strategies are not only ineffective, but they are *harmful* as well:

Cooperation

Noncooperation without resistance

Making a moral appeal

Crying

Pleading

No strategy

The following are strategies that are *effective:*

Yelling

Resistance with physical force

Fleeing/running

Immediate, active, and forceful resistance is the best means of avoiding rape. The more tactics you use, the better.

Strategies for Countering an Assailant With a Weapon

Research agrees that the outcome of the encounter is determined more by the actions and determination of the resister, rather than whether or not the assailant has a weapon. However, we still need to be concerned with the fact that guns and knives are lethal weapons. We will discuss your options and strategies in LESSON EIGHTEEN: Physical Defense—Defense Against Weapons.

Physical Resistance and Injury

If you resist, you have your best chance of getting away safely. You have a choice of surrendering or resisting. If you surrender, the least that will happen to you is that you will be raped. To be raped is to suffer extreme psychological injury— damage to your self-esteem and integrity as a human being that may last a lifetime. Whoever says that "rape is only sex" is an insensitive and stupid lout. If you surrender, the attacker can do whatever he wants to you. This may include the unthinkable. In addition, you need to be concerned about AIDS.

In the studies described in *Exploding The Myth of Self-Defense,* researchers found that although physical resistance often results in minor injury, such as bruises and scratches, most individuals do get away safety. No resistance guarantees rape and possible further injury, or death.

Two days ago, I read an article in the police and courts section of my local newspaper. The article talked about a 17-year-old girl who was walking in town at 10:40 P.M. when a man pulled his car over, asked for directions, then offered her a ride. When she declined, he jumped out of his car and tried to grab her. Typically, the young woman would be blamed for the attack. "Why was she out by herself late at night?" one might ask. The typical outcome might have been kidnapping and rape and perhaps murder. Not this young woman. She kicked the assailant in the groin and ran away. The paper reported that the police were looking for a balding, overweight man with a pot belly and a chubby face. Good for her!!! Good for all of us that fight back!

The Difference Between Victim and Resister Behavior

As discussed in LESSON THREE, the assailant tests his potential victim prior to attacking. If she flunks the intimidation test, he will attack. In his classic study of rape resistance and victimization, Dr. James Selkin reported the behavioral differences between the two groups.[1] Selkin studied 32 women who were raped and 23 women who successfully resisted rape. He found clear-cut differences in the way rape victims and resisters felt and behaved during the assault. The big difference was that resisters experienced rage and anger, and their emotional state provoked outcry and action; as a result they were not raped. Victims experienced emotions akin to physical and mental paralysis when confronted by assailants. They experienced shock and terror; they froze, panicked, and behaved submissively during the assault.

These differences are demonstrated by two women under similar circumstances. The first woman was working alone in a small shop when, at closing time, with no customers in the shop, a man walked in and handed her a card that read. "I have a gun. Do not make a sound. Come into the back room with me and do as I say or I will kill you." Paralyzed with fear, the woman meekly went into the back room and was raped. The second woman was at work in the shop when, several weeks later, the man returned near closing time and approached with the same card. "You have some nerve coming in here!" she yelled. "You bastard, get the hell out of here!" Taken aback, the would-be rapist fled. The woman who was raped suffered serious psychological trauma and experienced such severe anxiety, nightmares, and depression that after a year she left the country.

I have spoken both to rape survivors and to counselors, and both groups have told me that during the rape, the victim often feels detached from her body. I have a theory which may explain this—and the solution to prevent this detachment from happening. During the testing phase, the goal of the predator is to strike fear into the heart of his prey. He must intimidate his victim or he will not be able to accomplish what he wants. He needs someone who will display quiet, orderly, cooperative behavior. I believe that the detachment comes as a result of becoming paralyzed with fear. When you freeze, your systems shut down. When your systems shut down, your breathing is slow and shallow. When this happens, very little oxygen gets to your brain. When you don't have enough oxygen, your conscious state is altered. The solution to this is raging (See "raging" in LESSON THREE). Raging prevents the paralysis behavior from ever happening. When you get angry and start to yell viciously, this triggers adrenaline into your bloodstream, and the flow of oxygen to your brain. You will also transform so that your force field of fury will push the assailant away. As an additional benefit, you will temporarily develop tremendous strength.

Key Points To Remember

1. The following rape resistance strategies are not only ineffective, but they are harmful as well:

Cooperation
Noncooperation without resistance
Making a moral appeal
Crying
Pleading
No strategy

2. The following strategies are effective:
Yelling
Resistance with physical force
Fleeing/running

NOTES

1. James Selkin, "Protecting Personal Space: Victim and Resister Reactions to Assaultive Rape," *Journal of Community Psychology,* 1978, No. 6, pp. 263-268.

LESSON EIGHT
Physical Defense—Releases: Grabs

Your object is to get away safely. If an assailant is attacking you, it is best to prevent him from reaching you by blocking and/or moving out of the way or by breaking out of his hold. Then immediately counterattack a vulnerable target area, yell, incapacitate him, and run away. These are techniques to use to break out of situations where you are being grabbed.

When Grabbed by the Wrist

The most vulnerable area on someone grabbing your wrist is the upper knuckle area of his thumb. In breaking out of a wrist grab, direct your force into this area. As in any defense, your response must be immediate. Get into your stance, yell, and forcefully break out of the grab. Note: If any wrist grab defense does not work, immediately kick the attacker in the knee or use another counterattack.

One-Handed Grab

If possible, grab the fist of the arm being held (Figure 32). If the assailant's thumb is on top, grab your own fist from the top; if his thumb is underneath, grab your fist underneath. Using the power coming from your legs as well as your arms, forcefully twist into the direction of his upper thumb joint (Figures 32 and 33). If you feel that you need more leverage for an effective release, move your feet to get into a better position. Make sure to yell. Counterattack with a kick to the kneecap if you are kicking distance away, or, if you are within punching distance, attack the Adam's apple.

Two-Handed Grab

It is not exactly smart for an assailant to grab you with two hands—both his hands are being used. Take advantage of this situation by kicking him in the kneecap. If he steps back, use his hold for leverage, step forward and kick. As always, yell.

FIGURE 31.
One-handed grab:
assailant grabs wrist

FIGURE 32.
Grabbing own wrist

FIGURE 33. One-handed grab release: grab is forcefully broken

When Grabbed by the Arm

Use the same principles to break an arm grab as a wrist grab— break into the upper joint of the assailant's thumb. If he has come from behind and grabbed your arm (Figure 34), pivot toward him and break out of the grasp, using the same upward and outward motion you would use in an upward block (Figure 35). Your counterattack options are the same as for the one-handed grab. If the attacker has grabbed both of your arms from the rear, use the back kick to break his hold (Figure 15).

FIGURE 34. (above)
Arm grab release:
assailant grabs arm from behind

FIGURE 35. (below)
Arm grab release:
breaking from grasp

When Grabbed by the Hair

If you have long hair and the assailant grabs it, put your hand between his hand and your scalp. If you have short hair, put both your hands over the assailant's hands and press down. In both cases this will help alleviate the pain. Do not attempt to pull away from him. Rather, move toward him and attack with a kick to the knee, a punch in the throat, or a jab to the eyes.

Practice Drills

1. This is an excellent drill which gives you practice in both the skill of breaking out of an arm grab from the rear and the psychological practice of sending out the "Don't mess with me!" signal. Start walking. You partner will then run up from behind, catch you by surprise, and hassle or threaten you. You forcefully pivot toward him, using an upward block and finishing in your stance (Figure 35). Yell, at the top of your lungs, "Get away from me!" or "Get out of here!" Your aim is to, in essence, blow the assailant away from you using your force field of fury. Your partner will let you know how convincing you are. Practice until you are convincing. If the attacker is not immediately gone, be prepared to incapacitate him.

2. In practicing, make sure that you grab each other's wrists tightly. If you don't, you will not know whether your release has been effective. Practice different angles, and different grabs.

Key Points to Remember

1. Immediately get into a stance for power and balance.
2. Break out of a grab immediately. Don't give the assailant a chance to get entrenched.
3. Twist into the thumb joint to ensure that your release will be effective.
3. Remember to yell.

LESSON NINE
Assault Prevention—Known Assailants

Scope of the Problem

Acquaintance rape accounts for the overwhelming number of sexual assaults, yet it is the least reported of all. The legal definition of rape, as defined by the U.S. Department of Justice is: "...the carnal knowledge of a female forcibly and against her will. Assaults or attempts to commit rape by threat of force are also included; however, statutory rape (without force) and other sex offenses are excluded."[1] The definition of sexual assault as found in the California Penal Code is more encompassing. Sexual assault is: "any involuntary sexual act in which a person is threatened, coerced, or forced to comply against his/her will."[2]

Acquaintance rape is a problem of epidemic proportions. Consider the following:

• Sixty percent of college-aged men said they would commit a rape if they knew they could get away with it[3].

• A 1987 survey in Rhode Island schools showed that one in four middle-school boys thought it was O.K. to force a girl to have sex if he spent more than $10 on her.

• Rape is the only brutal crime for which the public frequently blames the victim.

• No more than 5 percent of reported rapes actually results in conviction.[4]

Acquaintance rapists are, for the most part, not considered sick, and have the same psychological characteristics as the *man next door*.[5] Most rapes take place indoors[6] and are planned ahead of time.[7]

Teenagers are particularly vulnerable to rape by acquaintances, and often an adolescent is the victim of more than one attacker at a time. Frequently, the rape occurs during social occasions such as parties. Typically, the young woman is seeking friendship and peer acceptance and gets into a situation beyond her control.

The magnitude of acquaintance rape and the shocking reality of its widespread practice can be found on college campuses. The typical victim is a freshman and the typical rape is committed during the first few weeks of the school year—when the experience of going away to college is new. The predators are upperclassmen, who lie in wait. They know how to manipulate the young women, know what they can get away with, what to say and what moves to make.

Since *How To Fight Back and Win* is, above all, about solutions to problems, let us get to the issue of how to prevent acquaintance rape and of what to do if you are in a situation in which you need to escape. For more detailed information about the issue of acquaintance rape, see *Exploding the Myth of Self-Defense*, Chapter Five—Acquaintance Rape Avoidance and Defense.

Prevention

First, let us start by reiterating the concept of distance, as discussed in LESSON ONE. We think of self-defense in terms of keeping distance between you and someone who wants to harm you. You can conceptualize this strategy in terms of placing barriers between you and the assailant. The barriers can be physical or psychological or both. What we do then is to prevent the situation from occurring in the first place. This is always the best option.

Develop your self-esteem and self-respect

If you respect yourself, you demand that others respect you. You don't let others manipulate you or push you around. Remember, when you respect yourself, you believe in your own worth as a human being. You have the power to determine the course of your life and to make your own decisions. No one has the right to take your power away from you.

Whether or not you go out on a date or go to a party is a matter of choice. Personal power implies choice. What you must change is your level of awareness, and you must stay in control. Understand the entrapment game and refuse to play it. Then, you maintain control of your environment as well as your choices.

Prevent Entrapment

Acquaintance rape usually involves entrapment. The rapist manipulates his prey into an area in which she is alone with him and where he is not likely to be discovered. It is also a situation in which she is not likely to be believed. The game the rapist is playing is to manipulate you into a trap and the goal of the game is to score.

Do not allow yourself to be alone with anyone, unless you know him well enough to trust him implicitly. Avoid entrapment by refusing to play the game at all.

Trust your intuition. As discussed in LESSON THREE, developing your sixth sense and listening to it is one of the most important self-defense skills that you can learn. If you sense that something is wrong, it is. If an alarm sounds and you sense that something is not exactly right, then something is not exactly right. This feeling is more than enough for you to act. Your well-developed intuition will let you know when you can trust someone or when you can't.

Communicate clearly. In communicating with another person, make sure that your verbal and nonverbal messages don't contradict each other. If you say *No*, you must say it three ways. *No* is *no* with your eyes, *No* is *no* with your voice and *No* is *no* with your body language.

Suggestions for Avoiding the "Dating Game" Trap

- Meet in a public place.
- Provide your own transportation.
- Pay for part of the date.
- Listen to your intuition—your gut feelings.
- Ask questions; listen to and analyze what your date means or implies as well as what he says.
- If you are uncomfortable, end the date and leave.

Rape Avoidance and Defense Strategies

Even though you have taken all possible precautions to prevent an assault from happening in the first place, there are times when you may be caught in an uncomfortable, risky, or dangerous situation.

Suppose you are in an isolated situation with an acquaintance and your intuition tells you that something is wrong, then you must pay attention—even if you feel mildly uncomfortable. Many women experience a delayed perception of the threat to them. Because of her failure to act immediately, a woman could find herself pinned down by the would-be rapist. It is very important for you to be able to read the signals and take immediate action before he physically attacks.

Graduated Responses

The acquaintance rapist does not want to be caught in the act of raping. Therefore, the first thing to do when you read his signals is to order him to stay away from you. Use direct eye contact, a forceful voice, and aggressive body language. Command, "Don't take one step closer!," or "Stop, don't touch me!," or "Get away from me!" You might also choose to put your arm and hand out in a stop signal.

If he doesn't get the message and stop, you need to be more forceful. Get angry and furious. Create a force field of fury. Yell at him to get away from you and leave you alone. At this point, you may chose to create a very loud, noisy scene. Remember, the rapist doesn't want to get caught. He wants an easily intimidated victim, not a screaming, furious madwoman! He doesn't want any evidence of a struggle or fight—so start breaking things, and throwing things around the room. Dishes, for example, make a nice mess. Broken and bent lamps are embarrassing. Broken mirrors and windows are hard to hide.

If the situation precludes physical resistance or if you are pinned down, trick the assailant. Your object here is to escape his physical control. Therefore, you must trick the assailant into believing one thing, and then do something else. One example of a ruse is to tell him that you need to use the bathroom to freshen up. A better one is to get him to use the bathroom. He will fall for these tricks if he believes that you are intimidated into doing what he wants. You must keep your mind functioning clearly and keep telling yourself that you are going to stop him and get away safely. Observe everything. Look for escape routes. Once you are out of his physical control, you may be able to escape.

If the situation worsens and if you need to fight back physically, then by all means do so. Remember, this man is trying to rape you. He is trying to rob you of your dignity and integrity as a human being. He has no right to do this. So go ahead, transform into a force field of fury, attack and incapacitate him.

Key Points To Remember

1. Acquaintance rapists are, for the most part, not considered sick, and have the same psychological characteristics as the *man next door.*

2. Prevention entails developing your self-esteem and self-respect.

3. Prevent entrapment

4. Use graduated responses to thwart an attack

NOTES

1. U.S. Department of Justice, "Crime in the United States," *Uniform Crime Reports,* 1990.
2. San Francisco State University, *Sexual Assault Policy,* May, 1991.
3. Valerie Frankel, "Why Rape Statistics Don't Add Up," *Mademoiselle Magazine,* December, 1991.
4. Subcommittee on Domestic and International Scientific Planning, Analysis and Cooperation, *Research into Violent Behavior: Overview and Sexual Assaults,* U.S. Government Printing Office, 1978.
5. Andra Medea, and K. Thompson, *Against Rape,* Farrar, Straus and Giroux, 1974.
6. National Institute of Mental Health, *Victims of Rape,* U.S. Government Printing Office, 1978, 28.
7. Burt, in *Research into Violent Behavior,* p. 308.

LESSON TEN
Domestic Violence Prevention

Nature and Scope of the Problem

The issue of domestic violence and spousal abuse was brought into the forefront of people's minds in the summer of 1994 when Nicole Brown Simpson was murdered. In the ensuing trial, it was reported that O.J. Simpson, the football star, battered his wife. Another form of abuse against women became the subject of public discussion.

Who is a Battered Woman?

A battered woman is defined as one "...who is repeatedly subjected to any forceful physical or psychological behavior by a man in order to coerce her into doing what he wants without regard for her rights as an individual. The battered woman perceives that she has no control over the batterer's behavior. Battered women include wives and women in any form of intimate relationship with men."[1]

Bureau of Justice Statistics Report

The following information from the U.S. Bureau of Justice Statistics, clearly demonstrates the magnitude, prevalence, and horrific nature of domestic violence.[2]

In a November 1994 report, the U.S. Bureau of Justice Statistics (BJS) reported on violence between intimates. The information that follows in this section comes from this report. The crimes reported here include those murders, rapes, robberies or assaults which are committed by spouses, ex-spouses, boyfriends, or girlfriends. The BJS admits that violence between intimates is difficult to measure because it often occurs in private, and victims are often reluctant to report incidents because they are ashamed or fear reprisals. However, enough information is available to shed light on the magnitude of this issue.

Assault

Most violence between intimates is assault. In 1992, 81% of the violent victimizations committed by spouses and ex-spouses were assault.

Murders

Of the 22,540 murders committed in the United States in 1992, 61% of the murderers knew their victims. Approximately 15% of the murders involved a relationship described in police records as intimate.

Gender

Women are much less likely than men to become victims of violent crimes in general, but are over ten times more likely than males to be victims of violence by intimates.

Reporting

Approximately 20% of females victimized by their spouse or ex-spouse reported to the National Crime Victimization Survey (NCVS) in 1992 that they had been a victim of a series of 3 or more assaults in the last 6 months.

Weapons

For rape, robbery, and assaults recorded in the NCVS, 18% of the women victimized by intimates were threatened by an armed assailant. (This compares to 33% of those victimized by strangers.) 40% of these threats involved knives, 34% involved guns, 12% involved blunt objects, and 15% involved other weapons. However, in 1992, 62% of the murder victims who were killed by intimates were shot to death. Over three-quarters of the firearms used to kill intimates were handguns.

Spousal murder

The following are characteristics of spousal murder cases in urban areas:

Time and place of the murder

One third of the spousal murders and a quarter of non-spousal murders were committed during the day. Close to 86% of victims who were killed by spouses and 20% of nonfamily members were murdered at home.

Victim involvement

Over 23% of the murdered intimates precipitated the incident by provoking the murder with a deadly weapon, with a nonlethal weapon, or with physical contact such as punching or pushing.

Alcohol use at the time of murder

Over half of the accused murderers had been drinking alcohol at the time of the crime. Also, almost half of the victims had also been drinking at the time of the murder.

Gender

A study of murder cases in large urban counties in 1988 revealed: almost 60% of defendants who killed their spouses are male, 77% were over age 30. Defendants who murdered nonfamily members were 93% male and 65% under the age of 30.

Police response to domestic disputes

Most police agencies and sheriffs' departments in the United States have written policies concerning domestic disturbances. In large urban areas, special units to deal with domestic violence are utilized by over 40% of the law enforcement agencies.

In 1992, 14 states and the District of Columbia had laws requiring arrest in crimes of domestic violence. These states include: Arizona, Connecticut, Hawaii, Iowa, Louisiana, Maine, Missouri, Nevada, New Jersey, Oregon, Rhode Island, South Dakota, Washington, and Wisconsin. In order to arrest a suspect, police are required to obtain an arrest warrant from a judge before arresting a suspect unless they are able to show at the time of the arrest they had probable cause to believe the suspect had committed the crime. Warrantless probable-cause arrests in cases of domestic violence are authorized in 47 States and the District of Columbia. Most state codes permitting warrantless arrests for domestic violence crimes also instruct police to inform victims of certain rights, including the availability of protection order, shelter or emergency facilities, and transportation.

The following information is from the U.S. Bureau of Justice Statistics Violence Against Women Report.[3]

Race

White and black women experienced equivalent rates of violence by intimates and other relatives.

Education

Women with lower education and family incomes levels were more likely to be victimized by intimates than women who had graduated from college and who had higher family incomes.

Location
There was no difference in rates of violence between women living in rural, suburban or urban areas.

Injury
Women suffering violent victimizations were almost twice as likely to be injured if the offender was an intimate.

Self-defense
Over half of the women who tried to protect themselves against offenders who were intimates believed that their self-protective behavior helped the situation. Almost a quarter of the women believed their actions actually made the situation worse. [I question whether these women had self-defense training. If so, the outcomes may have been different.]

Cycles of Violence

Lenore Walker describes the cycles of violence. She found a well-established, three phase pattern of battering within an abusive relationship. The following is a summary of her findings.

Phase One—Tension Building Phase
"Tension begins to rise and the woman can sense the man becoming somewhat edgy and more prone to react negatively to frustrations. This can include little episodes of violence. ...Thus he may begin to lash out verbally and quickly apologize."[4] The woman tries to calm the man. She denies feeling angry or afraid. She feels powerless. He becomes more and more jealous and possessive. He fears that she will leave him because she knows his behavior is not appropriate. She withdraws more and more. The minor incidents increase, and the tension becomes unbearable.[5]

Phase Two—Acute Battering Incident

The man loses control over his behavior and acutely batters the woman. He tries to justify his behavior by blaming her. He doesn't remember much of the incident; she does. The attack is usually followed by shock, denial and disbelief. Both people try to rationalize. She is under severe psychological stress—loss of appetite or overeating, fatigue, headaches, insomnia, etc. Women do not usually seek help during this phase unless they are badly hurt. They usually return to their partners after being treated in the emergency room.[6]

Phase Three—Kindness and Contrite Loving Behavior

He knows he went too far and tries to make it up to her. This is a period of unusual calm. He is sorry, begs forgiveness, and promises never to do it again. She wants to believe him. She sees how wonderful he can be. He reminds her of how much he needs her. He is sincere and believes he can control himself. Each is dependent upon the other and bonding occurs. Both want to make their relationship work.[7] Then, Phase One repeats.

Why Women Stay

Women stay because they love the man. In addition, they stay for economic reasons or they fear being killed or they fear receiving more serious injuries if they attempt to leave. They stay to keep the family together, and they stay because they are afraid of change.

In addition to the above reasons, many battered women are embarrassed and do not want to air their dirty laundry. They have been traditionally socialized and believe that their role is to be secondary to that of the male. Above all, I believe that the main cause for women to stay in this type of relationship is low self-esteem.

Prevention

Prevention, as always, is your best defense. Staying out of a battering relationship is so much better than trying to extract yourself from one.

How to Identify a Potential Batterer

Recognizing the characteristics of batterers may help you avoid getting into an abusive relationship. Becoming aware of violent patterns is the first step toward either prevention or change.

Characteristics of Batterers

The following characteristics of batterers come from a handout adapted from Project for Victims of Family Violence, Fayetteville, Arkansas.[8]

Jealousy
Jealous of time you spend with others

Controlling Behavior
Doles out money, angry if you are late
Keeps you away from friends or family

Quick Involvement
Rushes you into an engagement or marriage

Unrealistic Expectations
Expects you to be everything to him
Blames others for his problems
Blames other for his feelings
Claims that you control how he feels

Hypersensitive
Is easily insulted

Cruelty to Animals or Children

Forced Sex

Verbal Abuse

Rigid Sex Roles
Believes women should serve and obey men
Believes that women are inferior to men and less
    intelligent
Refuses to cook, wash dishes, or take care of children

Past Battering

Jean Green, worked for over five years as a volunteer for an organization known as WOMAN, Inc. (Women Organized To Make Abuse Nonexistent.) In listening to victims of battery, Ms. Green heard the same recurring patterns and themes over and over again. Her approach is prevention. "Get to know the person as quickly as possible. Get past the information about jobs, favorite colors, where you enjoy vacationing, sports, etc.. These make nice conversation but count not at all in his/her treatment of you. Watch carefully all the interactions with others—the gas station attendant, waitress, and especially family. Ask questions. Check his behavior and attitude when confronted with a problem or stressful situation. Listen to what is said, how he talks about things, and where his anger lies.

"Do not tiptoe around afraid to be yourself and express your feelings. If you can't find out what you need to know by listening and looking, go one step further. Get the person angry! Just a little anger will tell you all you need to know. Does he yell, kick or throw things? Does he hurl insults or profanity? Does he become sullen, speak threateningly or vindictively?

Does he admit he has hit women in the past? Does he strike you? If so, get out of the relationship quickly, without looking back. If you don't, you will have your turn at being abused.[9]

Self-esteem

I cannot overemphasize the concept of self-esteem, the love of yourself. This theme has run throughout all of my teaching in self-defense, from 1981 when *Are You A Target?* was first published, to the publication of *Exploding The Myth of Self-Defense*, to 1995 in the first edition of *How to Fight Back and Win—The Joy of Self-Defense*. The following quote is from the preface of *Are You A Target?*

"This book is about freedom. Its purpose is to help you gain the knowledge, insights, and courage to make the necessary changes in your life to become a successful assault resister. You are born neither a victim nor a resister. But many of us become conditioned to behave passively when threatened with physical and/or sexual assault, and we agree to become victims.

You don't have to be a victim. Being a resister means that you make deliberate choices, you make conscious decisions, you have control. Being a resister means that, under a given set of circumstances, you decide to do what you believe is in your best interest and determine not to have that power and control taken away from you."[10]

Self-defense begins with self-esteem, i.e., the belief in oneself. You must believe that you are worth fighting for. In order to develop personal power, you must learn to believe in your own sanctity as a human being. You are a unique, worthwhile person. You respect yourself, and thus others respect you. You have the fight to live your life the way you choose. No one has any right to try to take your integrity away from you. No one has the right to touch you without your consent. No one has the right to hurt you!

Take steps to increase your self-esteem. If you do not feel that you have good self-esteem, then take whatever steps that are necessary to achieve it. I would suggest taking a class in self-defense for women (if you are female.) This class must include both psychological and physical skills. My main goals in teaching self-defense for women are to empower women psychologically and to teach the skills so that they learn to protect themselves physically. I strongly recommend reading my book, *Exploding the Myth of Self-Defense—A Survival Guide for Every Woman.* This book is a primer in the development of personal power. It includes numerous success stories, including the story by a woman named Margo, who was in an abusive relationship. Margo's life completely changed as a result of the psychological changes she made during the self-defense class.

Check out the availability of women's support groups in your areas. Information is available through battered women's shelters, through groups such as the Y.W.C.A., and through rape crises centers. If you decide to speak to a therapist or counselor, make sure that the individual you seek out has specific training in helping people in abusive relationships develop self-esteem.

How to Help a Friend

If you have a friend that you suspect of being battered or in an abusive relationship, let her know you care by listening. Learn as much as you can about domestic violence. Do not underestimate her fear of danger. Believe what she says and try to help her find a safe place by calling local hotlines and shelters.[11]

National U.S. Resources.

I am listing national resources. Most communities offer a variety of services, and most states have domestic violence coalitions. These will give you a start in the right direction. Remember to keep asking questions until you get the information or answers that you are looking for.

National Council on Child Abuse and Family Violence
800-222-2000

NOVA (National Organization for Victim Assistance
202-232-6682 or 800-879-6682 (crisis line)

Office for Victims of Crime Resource Center (U.S.
Department of Justice)
800-627-6872

National Victim Center
817-8777-3355

National Resource Center on Domestic Violence
800-537-2238

Battered Women's Justice Project
800-903-0111

Health Resource Center on Domestic Violence
800-313-1310

National Criminal Justice Reference Service
800-581-3420 or 800-732-3277

The Family Violence Prevention Fund (provides listing
of state domestic violence coalitions)
415-252-8900

Key Points to Remember

1. A battered woman is defined as one "who is repeatedly subjected to any forceful physical or psychological behavior by a man in order to coerce her into doing what he wants without regard for her rights as an individual."

2. The cycles of violence is a well-established three phase pattern of battering within an abusive relationship. Phase One is the tension building phase, Phase Two comprises an acute battering incident, Phase Three is the kindness and contrite loving behavior stage. These stages repeat.

3. Prevention, as always, is your best defense. Staying out of a battering relationship is so much better than trying to extract yourself from one.

4. Take whatever steps that are necessary to increase your self-esteem.

NOTES

1. Lenore E. Walker, *Who Are Battered Women?*, Unpublished paper, circa 1978.
2. U.S. Department of Justice, Bureau of Justice Statistics, Selected Findings, *Violence between Intimates*, NCJ-149259, November 1994.
3. U.S. Department of Justice, Bureau of Justice Statistics, *Violence Against Women*, January 1994, NCJ-145325.
4. Lenore E. Walker in *Who Are Battered Women?*
5. *Battered Women*, Harper & Row Publishers, 1979.
6. *Ibid.*
7. *Ibid.*
8. Handout adapted from Project for Victims of Family Violence, Fayetteville, Arkansas.
9. Jean Green, unpublished story.
10. Judith Fein, *Are You A Target?*, Torrance Publishing Co., 1988.
11. *What Every Woman Needs to Know about Violence Against Women*, booklet, Ryka ROSE Foundation, 1992.

LESSON ELEVEN
Physical Defense—Releases:
Choke Holds, Bear Hugs, and Rear Attacks

Choking Attack

Breaking a choking hold is relatively simple, and the same technique is used in attacks from the front or the rear. The principle to remember is to forcefully use your raised shoulders to break out of the hold. You must raise both arms, and the arms must be straight up in the air. Otherwise, it will not work.

Rear Choke Releases

If attacked from the rear (Figure 36), immediately get into your fighting stance. At the same time follow these steps:

1. Raise your arms directly over your head, reaching for the sky.

2. While you are raising your arms, forcefully pivot 180 degrees so that you are facing the attacker. (Pivot on the balls of your feet.) Keep your arms raised and your hands reaching for the sky until you have completely broken out of the hold (Figures 37 and 38).

3. Counter attack by gouging the attacker's eyes with your thumbs (Figure 39).

4. He will probably respond by trying to grab your wrists. As he does so, knee him in the groin (Figure 40).

Figure 36.
Rear choke release:
attacked from rear

Figure 37.
Rear choke release:
raising arms and pivoting

Figure 38.
Rear choke release:
hold broken

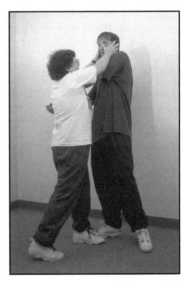

Figure 39.
Rear choke release:
eye gouge counterattack

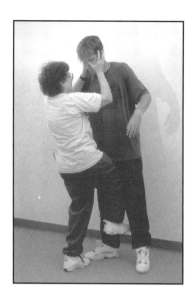

Figure 40.
Rear choke release:
knee to groin
counterattack

Front Choke Release

If attacked from the front (Figure 41), immediately get into your stance.

1. Raise your hands on the outside of his arms, directly over your head (Figure 42).

2. Forcefully pivot about 120 degrees (or until you have broken out of the hold but can still see the attacker) (Figure 43).

3. Counterattack with one of the following: an elbow to the throat (Figure 44); a finger jab to the eyes (see Figure 24); a punch to the Adam's apple (See Figure 25); or, if you are out of range, a side kick to his knee (See Figure 13).

Escaping a "Bear Hug"

Front Bear Hug

A bear hug occurs when an assailant grabs you from the front and pins your arms below the elbow (Figure 45). There are several responses which you can make. You can knee him to the groin, grab his testicles and squeeze, or use an upward hit to the groin.

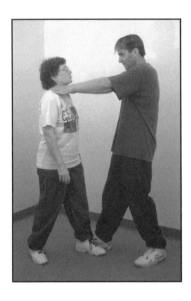 

Figure 41.
Front choke release:
attacked from front

Figure 42.
Front choke release:
arms raised

Figure 43.
Front choke release:
forceful pivot

Figure 44.
Front choke release:
elbow to throat counterattack

Figure 45.
Front bear hug

Rear Bear Hug

In the case of a rear bear hug (Figure 46), crouch down as low as possible in your stance, and thrust your buttocks back into the assailant as hard as possible (Figure 47). This will cause him to lean forward, giving you some space to move. Immediately pivot to your side and slam your elbow into his stomach (Figure 48); then punch his Adam's apple (See Figure 25). An alternative would be to stomp down as hard as possible on his instep (Figure 49).

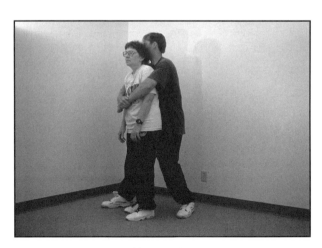

Figure 46.
Rear bear hug

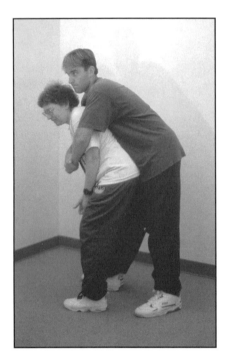
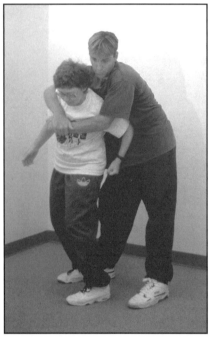

Figure 47. Rear bear hug: buttocks thrust hard into assailant

Figure 48. Rear bear hug: elbow blow to the stomach

Figure 49. Rear bear hug: smash to instep

Release from Rear Attack

Forearm Around Throat

One arm is around your shoulder, the other is over your mouth, or both arms are around your shoulder. He may try to pull you backward.

Option one

1. Immediately get into your stance. At the same time, turn your chin into the crook of his elbow to keep your air supply (Figure 50).

2. Using leverage and the power from your stance, break the hold by pushing up with your palm under the elbow of the arm which is around your neck. At the same time, pull down on the hand of his same arm (Figure 51).

Figure 50. Rear attack, forearm around throat: getting into the stance

Figure 51. Rear attack, forearm around throat: using leverage to break the hold

3. Utilizing the right angled space that you have created and holding on to his elbow and hand, duck down and turn in toward his body (Figure 52).

4. You are now behind the assailant. Break his elbow by holding the elbow steady with one hand, and pulling up and back on his hand (Figure 53).

5. Finish the counterattack by kicking him in the side or back of the knee and striking him in the back of his neck with the side of your forearm.

Figure 52. Rear attack, forearm around throat: turning in behind assailant

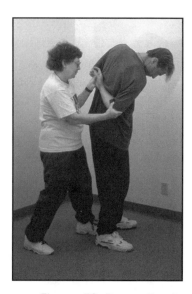

Figure 53. Rear attack, forearm around throat: breaking assailant's elbow

Option two

1. Immediately get into your stance. At the same time, turn your chin into the crook of his elbow to keep your air supply (See Figure 50).

2. Reach back with your hand on the same side that he is grabbing you and tap his leg. This is so you know exactly where his foot is (Figure 54).

3. Utilizing tremendous force and speed, stomp down on the instep of his foot (Figure 55).

4. As he loosens his grip, turn in to him and elbow him to the throat (Figure 56).

Figure 54. Rear attack, forearm around throat: tapping his leg

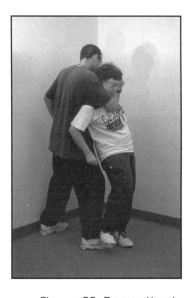

Figure 55. Rear attack, forearm around throat: stomping down on attacker's instep

Figure 56. Rear attack, forearm around throat: elbowing attacker in the throat

Release from Rear Garrote Attack.

You must instantly react to this extremely dangerous attack because it will be only moments before your air is cut off. The most important consideration is to protect your air supply.

1. The second you feel a thong strangling you, pivot forcefully toward the assailant, keeping your arms down at your sides. The pressure will then be on the bony part of your neck rather than on the soft tissue.

2. Immediately gouge the assailant's eyes, knee him in the groin, and smash down on the back of his neck. Do this viciously and forcefully.

Practice Drills

1. Have your partner grab you firmly. Know which skill you will be practicing. By surprise. Break the hold and counterattack.

2. Have your partner grab you firmly and by surprise, break the hold and counterattack.

Key Points to Remember

1. Rear attacks are surprise, dangerous attacks. Keep alert to prevent such an attack from occurring.

2. When you practice the choke hold, ask your partner to grasp your collar bone (rather than your neck.) You will be able to practice the release, safely utilizing a firm grasp.

3. Make sure to immediately get into your stance. To make sure your pivot is effective in the choke release, one foot must be forward, the other back.

4. In the rear attack with forearm around throat, not only must you immediately get into your stance, but you must also immediately turn your head into the crook of the elbow to preserve your air supply.

LESSON TWELVE
Streetwise Safety Strategies

Keep Alert in Public

This is your No. 1 secret in staying safe on the streets. In just about every attack that has taken place in public, reported to me over the past 22 years, the victim has been taken by surprise. How do I know this? I simply ask the individual the following question: "Where did the assailant come from?" The answer is always the same: "Nowhere" or "I don't know." Since assailants target people who are not paying attention, awareness is always your first step to prevent assault in public. In public includes everywhere outside your home. This not only means on the streets, it means when taking mass transportation or while you are driving your car.

Acquire Street Smarts

During one of my self-defense classes, we were discussing the concept of being hassled in public. I conducted an informal survey and asked my students how often they were bothered in public. Since the class was taking place in an urban area, I suspected that there would be more incidents than in a small town. Just about everyone had been hassled at least once over the past year, and many students had been bothered at least once during the past month. This is bad enough. Then one young woman stated that she was harassed almost every time she got on the bus. It turned out that she recently moved to the city from a rural area. Some people on the bus looked strange to her so she stared at them. This action drew them to her. "What are you looking at?!!!" would be a common reaction. This young woman got a crash course in street smarts.

Developing street smarts is an art. It involves knowledge of your surroundings and the ability to skillfully navigate even through the roughest waters.

Clothing

Your goal is to blend as much as possible with the local population. Of course, your choice of clothing depends on your activity and your sense of style. If, however, you look very different than everyone else, you will draw attention to yourself. If you wear shoes that prevent you from moving quickly, then you are hindering your ability to fight and to run if you need to. If you are walking through an economically disadvantaged area and wear the equivalent of the crown jewels, then you are in trouble. The point that I am making is that you do not want to stand out in public.

Routes

Be familiar with your routes. If you get lost, certainly don't act the part by pulling out a street map or asking directions of people on the streets. If your body language indicates that you don't know where you are, you make yourself vulnerable to being targeted. Go to a safe area to check your directions.

Alert Body Language

When you are in public, your body language indicates that you are alert, that you know where you are going, that you know what you are doing, and that you respect yourself. Under everyday circumstances, you send out a form of radar. This means that you know what is going on around you. You take a quick look at people and look around the area.

If You Cannot Blend

If you do look different than the rest of the local population, then what you do, as street-smart students in my self-defense class describe it, is to have an attitude. This means that you heighten your level of awareness and display no nonsense body language.

If You Are a Tourist or In an Unfamiliar City

When I asked my self-defense class how a tourist or person in a strange city ought to dress, they said to wear clothing appropriate to the weather. For example, a visitor to San Francisco who wore shorts in the summer would stand out like a sore thumb. This is because San Francisco is cold and foggy in the summer. In addition I recommend not wearing a camera or walking around with a map.

When to Use the "Don't mess with me" Signal

If you consider the situation dangerous, then navigate the streets sending out *Don't mess with me* signals. Under these circumstances, it is perfectly acceptable to stare at someone who may be looking at you. Your walk is brisk. You look around, and your body language indicates stay away from me.

How to Fight Street Harassment

As you develop street smarts you will come a long way in heading off the possibility of being harassed in the street. A keen sense of awareness and no nonsense body language will usually prevent you from being the target of a potential harasser. If you are harassed, the following techniques will help you maintain control and help keep your self-esteem.

Daytime Public Verbal Harassment

If someone grunts, whistles, gestures or jeers at you, I recommend that you consider the source. If you are not in physical danger, I suggest intentionally disregarding his presence. This type of non-response has two goals. The first is to help you stay calm and centered and able to continue your day without the disruption of an adrenaline rush. The second goal is not to acknowledge that this person exists. He desires and expects a response. Don't give him what he wants. Instead, keep a normal stride and assume a poker face.

Daytime Public Physical Harassment

Again, street smarts combined with a keen sense of awareness will prevent this from happening most of the time. Yet there are times when you are in a crowd or on a crowded elevator, and this individual will strike. This goal is a quick strike and then either a quick getaway, or the assumption of a poker face and plea of innocence or denial. If you catch him in the act, use a forceful block to slam him off of you. (See LESSON SIX—Physical Defense—Basic Skills: Blocking and Counterattacking.) Then create a big scene in public by yelling at him at the top of your lungs: "Get your hands off me you filthy pervert!"

Street Harassment in Dangerous Circumstances

Verbal or physical harassment in an unsafe area is not street harassment. It is a threat from a potential assailant. It is the testing phase of target—test—attack. Your appropriate behavior in this instance is to send out very strong *don't mess with me* signals to convince the assailant to leave you alone. These signals include very clear verbal and body language messages. If the attack is physical, respond with both psychological and physical self-defense techniques.

Strategies for Automatic Teller Machine (ATM) Safety

I do not recommend using ATMs. I consider them unsafe and a possible set-up for robbery. Since ATMs are a convenience, and are used throughout the world, we need to consider ATM safety.

Consider the case of two women. The first woman went to an ATM in a small city. She was aware and noticed that a car was parked nearby with its engine running. Although she decided to use the ATM, the woman looked directly at the two occupants of the car. Her body language and her eye contact indicated that she was aware of their presence and they had better stay back. A few minutes later, a second woman approached the ATM. She felt distracted and hurried. She did not notice the car with the engine running. She did not notice as the two men got out and approached her. She only noticed when she was mugged!

Therefore, your number one safety goal when using an ATM is to be aware of your surroundings. It is better to go to an ATM in daylight or, if you have to go at night, to one that is in a busy area, if possible, and is well-lit. One solution is to find a store, such as a 24 hour grocery store, that has an ATM right inside the store. It is also a good idea to bring a friend at night. This is so that, using the buddy system, one can use the ATM and the other can serve as a look-out and guard.

Taking Mass Transportation

The same general principles apply on mass transportation or on the streets— awareness is always your first step to prevent assault in public. Just as on the streets, you need to blend as much as possible with the population. You don't want to stand out.

While Waiting for the Bus or Train

Avoid isolation and darkness and be alert. If you are by yourself, I suggest standing with your back to a wall or barrier, so that you can see around without being surprised. If you consider the situation to be dangerous, send out *Don't mess with me* signals.

On the Bus

Sit closer to the driver rather than in the back of the bus. Sit on the outside seat if there are two seats across. This will prevent you from being trapped. Stay alert. If you are carrying a book bag or backpack, take it off and keep it between your legs. Glance at other passengers from time to time so that you know what is going on around you, but do not stare at anyone. Do not wear headphones to listen to a tape recorder or radio. This will signal that you are not aware. Avoid becoming engrossed in reading matter and above all do not fall asleep. Your job is to be aware and pay attention. Guard your valuables.

Car Safety and Carjacking Prevention

The same rules apply on your car or on the street. Pay attention. Carjackers, like all assailants, target individuals who are not aware and who can be taken by surprise.

Personal Safety Equipment

One piece of safety equipment that I recommend that you carry in your car is a portable cellular phone. The price of this piece of equipment has come way down in recent years. With a cellular phone you can easily summon help in an emergency without getting out of your car.

A second piece of safety equipment that I suggest is carrying a miniature high intensity flashlight. We will discuss its uses in this section. Another item to consider owning is a detachable keyring. This will permit you to detach your gas key or keep your car keys separate from your other keys.

Before Entering Your Car

Have your key ready and in your hand. This will prevent being taken by surprise while you are searching in your purse or pocket. Be alert and look around. Then look in the back and make sure no one is there. If it is dark, use the miniature high intensity flashlight for this purpose. Do this before you get in.

Upon Entering Your Car

Immediately lock your doors and windows. Leave nothing on the seats or in view that would attract attention—such as a purse.

When Purchasing Gasoline

It is best to detach your gas key from your other keys. Lock your doors and windows and take your keys with you. I suggest choosing a station that has a quick pay feature. This allows you to pay with a credit card without leaving the vicinity of your car. If you are in an urban area, pull up to the pumps which are closest to the attendant. Pay attention to your surroundings while you are putting gasoline in the tank.

Parking and Getting Out of Your Car

In an urban area, it is best to park in a high-trafficked area rather than on a quiet street. If it is, or will be, nighttime when you return to your car, park under a light. If you choose to park in a parking lot or garage make sure it is attended and park in a lighted area. Park as close to the attendant as you can, and in view of the attendant if possible. Leave nothing in view in the inside of the car. If you must leave packages, lock them in the trunk before you reach your final destination. Look before you get out of your car. If you intuitively don't feel comfortable, go elsewhere.

Carjacking Prevention

The idea here is to not get trapped, or taken by surprise. In areas that you consider dangerous, you may want to follow these additional safety precautions. I suggest that you keep your windows shut and your radio or tape deck turned to low. If a potential carjacker knows that you are listening to loud music, he knows that you are probably not paying attention. When you stop your car in traffic, stay in gear. Stop back far enough so that you can see the wheel of the car stopped in front of you. This is so that you can maneuver your car. Drive in an outside lane (as opposed to the curb lane where you could be boxed in). Above all, keep alert. Do not pick up hitchhikers. If you see someone in need of assistance and wish to help, dial 911.

If a car comes behind you and taps into you, assess the situation before taking action. If your intuition tells you that something is not right, take off. This is a typical carjacking ploy. You are not obligated to exchange driver's licenses with someone who taps you from the rear.

If someone or group of people approach your car, take off before they get there. (Here is where awareness pays off.) If you are surrounded, sound your horn and maneuver your car out of the situation. If you are trapped, as a last resort (unless you are threatened with a lethal weapon) roll down the window and spray the assailants with tear gas or pepper spray. (We will discuss this topic in LESSON NINETEEN: Physical Defense—Self-Defense Weapons.

Rental Cars

If you have rented a car, make sure that all rental identification is off the vehicle before you leave the parking lot. You may also wish to put your own bumper sticker on the rear bumper to disguise that it is a rental car. Figure out your routes before leaving the lot, so that you do not look like someone from out of town who is reading a map.

Key Points to Remember

1. Keep alert in public. This is your No. 1 secret in staying safe on the streets. Most people get attacked when they are not paying attention.

2. Developing street smarts is an art. It involves knowledge of your surroundings and the ability to skillfully navigate even through the roughest waters.

3. Carjackers, like all assailants, target individuals who are not aware. Do not get trapped, blocked in, or taken by surprise.

LESSON THIRTEEN
Physical Defense—Down Defenses

Basic Principles

A down defense describes defenses and counterattacks from a lying down position. Fighting from a down position is not my defense of choice. Not only are your movements limited, but you do not have the option of running away. Here your goal is to incapacitate the assailant as quickly as possible. You either do it before you knock him off you, or immediately afterwards. You then pick yourself up and run away.

If you are pinned down on your stomach, try to roll over onto your back. If this isn't possible, try to free an arm and punch him in the Adam's apple.

Falling Down Safely

First, train yourself to tuck in your chin. This will prevent whiplash and keep you from hitting your head on a hard surface. Next, learn to fall on either side of your buttocks, and tuck your wrist around your waist.

Attack first if possible. If you are knocked down, try to either kick the assailant in the groin or in the kneecap before he is on top of you (Figure 57).

Down Defenses

Assailant Straddling Across with Choke Hold

(Figure 58)

If you can reach, immediately jab your first and third fingers into his eyes. Then, you do two things at the same time—you break from the choke hold, and you thrust the

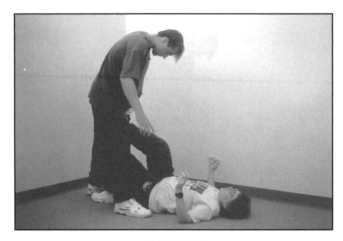

FIGURE 57.
Kicking assailant in groin from lying position

assailant off you. To break from the choke hold, use a double upward block with both your arms inside his arms (Figure 59). (See Figures 19 and 20 for the arm position of the upward block.) To thrust the assailant off of you, keep both knees bent, and both feet flat on the floor. Lift your hips and twist. Remember to coordinate the thrust with the breaking of the choke hold (Figure 60). The assailant will fly off of you. You then roll over, and punch him in the Adam's apple (Figure 61).

Assailant Straddling Across Pinning Arms Down
(Figure 62)

The technique for breaking out of this attack is almost the same as the choke hold attack. The main difference is that instead of breaking the choke hold, you thrust your arms straight back at the same time as you lift your hips (Figure 63).

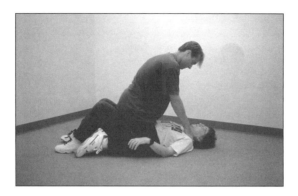

FIGURE 58. Assailant straddling across with choke hold

FIGURE 59. Breaking the choke hold and thrusting the hips

FIGURE 60. Thrusting assailant off

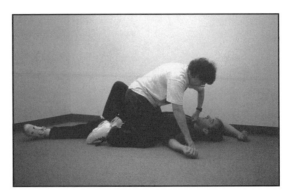

FIGURE 61. Counterattack to throat

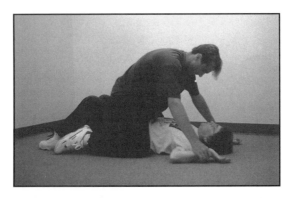

FIGURE 62. Assailant straddling across pinning arms down

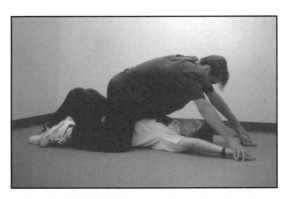

FIGURE 63. Breaking hold

Practice Drills

1. Practice falling on a mat or rug. Tuck your chin in, hold one arm across the front of your body, and land on your buttocks.

2. With a partner, take turns gently pushing each other down. Try to simulate kicking your partner in the groin or in the knee cap.

LESSON FOURTEEN
Protecting Your Home and Family—Mechanical Security and Psychological Barriers

Basic Concepts

When I first moved to the country after having grown up in New York City and spending fifteen years in San Francisco, I was shocked about the lack of security awareness that I found. I was brought up with street smarts and safety awareness. I knew to lock my doors; I automatically lock my car doors. A number of years ago, I went to visit a friend who was living in a suburban area. I arrived at the front door to find a note which said: "Hi, Judith. The door is unlocked, come on in. I am taking a shower." If you are thinking that only a stupid person would do such a thing, think again. Maybe most people wouldn't leave notes on the door, but most intruders get into homes by just walking in! They enter homes through unlocked doors and unlocked or open windows.

Your first and foremost level of defense is prevention. (Refer to Figure 2. The Three Levels of Defense and take a look at the outside circle.) If you want to protect yourself and your family you must think in terms of preventing intrusion. You do this through placing mechanical and psychological barriers between you and a potential intruder. Mechanical and psychological barriers, also known as physical security devices, will only keep intruders out if you utilize good safety awareness habits to back them up.

Mechanical Security

You want your home to be a safe place. The last thing you want to do is to wake up in the middle of the night and find an unwanted intruder standing over your bed. You prevent this nightmare from happening by taking security precautions. Then you can rest at ease. Your plan is threefold. First, if someone attempts to enter your prevention zone, you want psychological devices to ward them off. Second, you want mechanical barriers to keep criminals out. Third, if security is breached, you want to be warned, so that you are not taken by surprise.

Security Check From the Outside

Do this as an assignment. Walk down the block or street and pretend to be a burglar doing his/her homework. If you were to target potential houses for break-in, which ones would you choose and why? You will notice that some homeowners might as well put a "welcome burglar" mat at the front entrance. If you feel that this is your home, then I suggest taking steps to remedy the situation.

Just as on the streets, criminals target easy prey. They want an easy mark; they want to get into your home as quickly and easily as possible. They do not want to attract attention, and they do not want to be caught.

Defending the Perimeter

Chainlink fences are preferable to solid wooden fences because they afford less cover for a criminal. If your landscaping looks like it would make a good movie set for Sleeping Beauty's castle, where the vegetation grew for 100 years, then remember that this type of jungle provides excellent cover for criminals.

Bright lights are a deterrent to criminals. If a criminal walks into your yard and is lit up by floodlights, he may have second thoughts. The best types of lighting for this purpose are motion-detectors with photoelectric cells. These can be found in home supply stores and are easy to install. Purchase lights which are made of unbreakable plastic or are covered with wire mesh to prevent thieves from smashing out bulbs. They can be installed at entry points to the home, at garage doors, and under accessible windows. Garages need to be brightly lit and orderly. An intruder can easily sneak in and hide in a poorly lit garage. To prevent anyone from looking into your garage, either install light colored shades or whitewash the inside of garage windows. I also suggest putting a padlock on your outdoor electric box to deter criminals from turning off your electricity.

Mechanical Security

You prevent entrance by making it difficult for a criminal to just walk in. The more difficult you make it for the criminal, the less likely it is that he will gain entrance.

Marking your valuables

Property engraved with an identifying number is less likely to be stolen. Marked property is more difficult to sell because thieves can be more easily prosecuted if they are discovered with the stolen property in their possession and because identifying marks permit the police to return stolen property to their rightful owners. Check with your local police or sheriff as to what identifying marks or numbers they recommend. Many times, local police departments loan engraving tools to local residents and upon return of the tool, provide the user with a decal placed in windows around the house. The decal warns the potential intruder that items of value have been marked for ready identification by law enforcement agencies.

Video inventory

I suggest that you make a video survey of your home and its possessions. This includes audio descriptions as well as video. Make sure to take shots of any special collections and valuables that you have. Store the completed video inventory in your safe deposit box. You can update the tape either annually or when making a major purchase.

Doors

Sturdy, solid wooden doors are the best for security. Hollow-core doors are useless since they can be kicked through in seconds. Doors with glass panels can be reinforced with quarter-inch Plexiglas.

Oftentimes the door frame itself needs to be reinforced. A warped door, with a gap between it and its frame, or between the rough door frame and the finish frame, can be opened by an intruder with a pry bar. If such is the case, remove the finish frame and reinforce the rough frame with pieces of plywood secured to the rough frame with two-inch-long screws.

Doors with outside hinges

To secure a door with outside hinges, remove two middle screws from each leaf of the hinge. In one hole insert a strong screw or concrete nail and allow it to protrude half an inch. Drill out the other hole at least a half inch so the protruding screw opposite will be easily recessed in the hole when the door is closed (Figure 64).

The door which leads to the home from the garage is often flimsy and provided with inadequate locks. Be sure that this door is reinforced and is equipped with a deadbolt lock.

Sliding glass doors (and windows)

Your objective is to keep the door from sliding or being lifted up and out of its track. A length of dowel or a broomstick

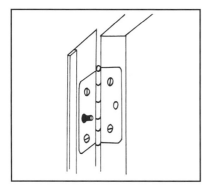

Figure 64. Securing a door with outside hinges

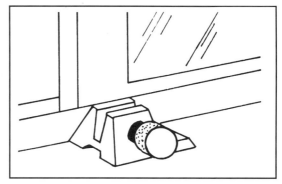

Figure 65. Slide bolt for security sliding glass door or window

in the track, by itself, offers little protection. In addition, you may wish to install a slide bolt (Figure 65). To keep the door from being lifted out of its track, drill holes in the upward tracks and install sheet metal screws. Screw them in enough for the door to still move on its tracks.

Pet doors

Pet doors could be an access point for an intruder if the size of the opening is large enough. Be aware of this if you choose to install a door for your pet(s).

The garage door

A single lock on the garage door is inadequate to keep a burglar from prying it up on the opposite side and crawling into the garage. Several methods may be used to reinforce this lock: (1) Add another bolt and padlock to the side opposite the lock; (2) add a top center hasp (made of hardened steel and installed with carriage bolts through the door); or (3) install a pair of cane bolts to the inside of the door.

Chains

They are easily broken through in seconds and are virtually useless as security devices. I consider door chains to be dangerous because they give the illusion of security.

Peepholes

Install an extra-wide angle viewer (with a 180 degree range). The peephole will permit you to look out but will prevent the person outside from looking in. Make sure that the area outside the front door remains lighted at night.

Locks

Every door that leads to the outside must have a deadbolt lock. Locks built into the door knob are flimsy and easy to pick. If your lock is insecure, install an auxiliary deadbolt lock with a one-inch bolt and hardened cylinder guard above your other lock. Use two-inch screws to secure the strike plate to the rough frame.

A deadbolt rim lock is installed on the inside of the door (Figure 66). The bolt can be either a one-inch deadbolt or the interlocking jimmy-proof variety. If glass is within forty inches of the lock, install a double cylinder lock. As a safety precaution, make sure to keep the key close (more than arm's reach) and visible.

Windows

Glass windows are obviously extremely vulnerable. A burglar could smash a window if he dared make the noise, and he could chisel away the putty if he dared take the time. (If your window putty is very old and fired out, a burglar could just lift the window out.) Windows at ground level are more vulnerable than those at higher levels, but determined intruders can use ladders, fire escapes , and trees to enter homes. Usually, the burglar will not risk smashing a window, but will look for a quiet and quick entry—easily accomplished by prying open a window or by opening an unlocked window or by entering through an open window!

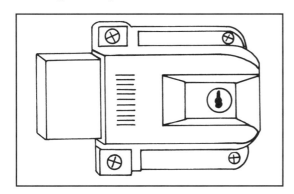

Figure 66.
Deadbolt rim lock

Double hung windows

A small crowbar placed between the sill and the lower window sash can develop a lifting force of a half ton. Therefore, locks commonly found on the market are not able to resist this type of force. What you can do, however, is drill a hole through the inside sash where it overlaps the top window three quarters of the way through the top window sash. Drill the hole at the downward angle and insert a 5/16-inch-diameter eyebolt. Do this on both sides of the window (Figure 67).

Windows can be locked in ventilating positions. This can be accomplished by screwing a quarter-inch screweye into the side tracks so that the window can be opened enough for ventilation but not enough to admit an intruder.

Casement windows

These are more difficult to break through than double hung windows. They are usually opened with a removable metal crank from the inside. For security, remove the crank when not in use and place it in a nearby drawer.

Louver windows

Louver windows are poor security risks; these should either be replaced with another type of window or be protected with an iron grate or grille.

Sliding glass windows

Secure them as you would sliding glass doors.

Windows at street level

Windows at street level and those facing fire escapes require additional protection as do basement windows. Security can be enhanced by the use of grilles, grates, or quarter-inch Plexiglas sheets. Ornamental bars that open from the inside will protect a window facing a fire escape. If you do not wish to utilize these devices, you may want to consider the use of alarms as a psychological barrier.

Psychological Barriers to Intrusion

Alarms

Alarms serve several purposes. They act as deterrents. If a potential burglar knows that you have an alarm system, he may be deterred enough to go somewhere else. He wants an easy target. He does not want to be caught in the act. If an intruder sets off an alarm, he will be startled, and most likely run away as fast as possible. In addition, the noise of an alarm will alert you so that you are not taken by surprise.

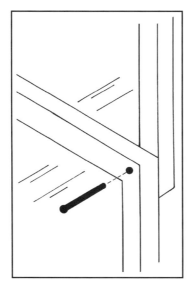

Figure 67. Securing a double hung window

Home alarm systems vary according to types, costs and services. You have the responsibility of determining your needs and budget. Alarms range from inexpensive portable alarms, which you can use for specific purposes, to complex monitored systems, which can also be integrated into a variety of home control systems. Alarms are either wireless or wired. Before you begin to shop for an alarm, assess your needs. Figure out what you want or need to protect. Simple systems can be purchased in home supply stores. If you choose to go with a complex system installed by a security company, go by referral and check the company's credentials. I would also suggest talking to friends and acquaintances who have security systems, so that you can discuss their experiences with these systems and, if applicable, the security company. Portable alarms will be discussed in LESSON SEVENTEEN: On the Road—Travel Safety.

Dogs

Dogs can be excellent deterrents to crime and also can sound the alarm for you. This is because they are territorial in nature. An alert dog will bark if anyone invades its territory. An intruder cannot know from the sound of a barking dog or from its looks, whether or not it is attack-trained. Either the sight or sound of a dog may be enough deterrent to cause a burglar to look elsewhere. A medium-size to large dog is probably best for both appearance and bark. If your house is entirely surrounded by a fence, a dog left outside can be a first line of alarm and protection. Otherwise, since the dog can't do anything to protect you if it is locked up in the backyard, I suggest leaving it inside when you are not at home, at night, and when a stranger is visiting.

Interior Lighting and Timers

Interior lighting will suggest that someone is inside; absence of interior lighting in the evening is a sure sign of an empty house. Timers can be installed on lights in various areas to give your home a lived-in look. Living rooms and bathrooms are good areas to light. Timers are also good on talk radio stations. The sound suggests that someone is home. Consider purchasing variable timers, so that lights do not go on and off at exactly the same time each day. You may also want to consider timers with multiple options.

Key Points to Remember

1. To be secure lock your doors and windows. Most intruders enter homes through unlocked doors and windows.

2. Every door that leads to the outside must have a deadbolt lock.

3. Interior lighting at night suggests that someone is inside.

4. Alarms act as deterrents and warn you of intrusion.

LESSON FIFTEEN
Escaping Multiple Attackers

Prevention

Your first defense has to be prevention. Multiple attackers present an extremely dangerous situation that you need to make every effort to avoid.

Know Your Area

Know as much as possible ahead of time about the area that you are going to be in. If you are forewarned about dangerous areas, you will be less likely to unwittingly traverse them. It is much better to go around a potential hot spot than to walk into a hornet's nest.

Be Aware

Keep alert to spot potential danger. Pay attention to your surroundings. If you notice people milling together, stay away.

Listen to Your Intuition

If you sense that something is wrong, it is. Immediately leave the area.

Carry a Non-lethal Aerosol Defense Weapon Such as C.S. Tear Gas or Pepper Spray

Canisters that hold fifteen or more seconds of these chemicals are extremely effective against more than one assailant. Do not hesitate to shoot the attackers in the face and then run. (Non-lethal weapons are discussed in detail in LESSON NINETEEN: Physical Defense—Self-Defense Weapons.)

Running Away

If you are alert, you may be able to run away. If you can pull off this option, then I suggest going for it. If you are in a commercial neighborhood, run into an open establishment. If nothing is open, yell "Fire!" as you run. If you are pursued, I suggest yelling, "Call the police!" and kicking in the glass of a storefront which has an alarm system. Criminals do not like the sound of breaking glass and do not want the police to arrive on the scene. It may not be legal to break glass storefronts, but I would rather explain my actions to the police and pay for the glass, than to end up in the hospital or worse.

If you are in a residential neighborhood, break away and yell "Fire!" as you run. I would run to a house that looks occupied, and break a window with a shoe or stone. If you go up to the house and ask for help, the chances are that nobody will help. People are afraid to get involved. If you break the glass, you can count on the police being called immediately.

If You Are Surrounded

Let us suppose you are surrounded. Try to ascertain what it is that the attackers want. If they want your valuables and/or your car, then give them to them. Remember, you cannot be replaced. However, if you believe that they want to physically attack or rape you, then this is a different matter.

How to Fight Back and Win

To fight back effectively, you must use a combination of both psychological and physical skills. I was once threatened by a gang of six men. I was attending an art festival in a large urban area and was taking pictures of some of the artwork.

Since I was intently checking my light meter and looking through the lens of the camera, I did not notice that six men had surrounded me. I certainly did not expect to be targeted. After all, it was a Sunday afternoon, and thousands of people were attending the festival. Yet I was targeted precisely because I was holding a valuable camera and light meter, and because I was not paying attention. I looked up as the six men circled closer like a pack of wolves. The leader snarled at me in an intimidating manner, questioning me about the value of my photographic equipment. I realized what was happening, and immediately transformed into a vicious beast. I yelled at the men and kicked at the leader. In essence, I created a force field of fury which pushed the circle back. The leader came in toward me again. I got into my karate stance and furiously yelled at them again. The six men ran away.

One of the things that I remember from this incident was how fast it all took place. I had to react without hesitation, and I had to react forcefully. I used a combination of both physical and psychological skills to fight off these attackers.

Fighting Back

If there are two or more attackers, usually one will grab you in order that the other(s) may have free rein to attack you (Figure 69). What must be done is as follows:

1. Determine which attacker is the most dangerous to you and deal with this person first. Usually, it is someone other than the person who is restraining you.

2. Use the attacker who is holding you for support and leverage, and kick the person who is coming in to attack you. Aim your attack at the knee (Figure 69). Then deal with the other assailant(s) in the same manner.

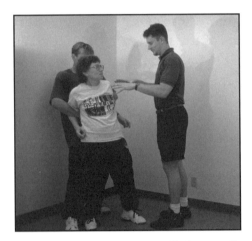

FIGURE 68. Release from multiple assailants:
one person acts to restrain

FIGURE 69. Release from multiple assailants:
kicking first assailant

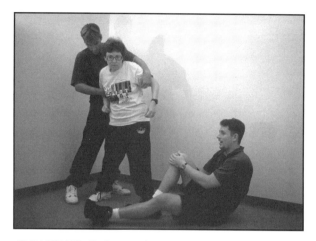

FIGURE 70. Release from multiple assailants:
attacking second assailant

3. The last one to consider is the person holding you. Break out of his grasp the same way you would handle an attack from the rear (See LESSON ELEVEN). Then incapacitate him (Figure 70). Of course, if you were being injured by him, you would act to incapacitate him first.

Key Points To Remember

1. Your first defense has to be prevention. Multiple attackers present an extremely dangerous situation that you need to make every effort to avoid.

2. If you are alert, you may be able to run away.

3. Use a combination of both psychological and physical skills if you choose to fight back.

LESSON SIXTEEN
Protecting Your Home and Family—
Safety Awareness Strategies

In LESSON FOURTEEN we discussed Protecting Your Home and Family—Mechanical Security and Psychological Barriers. As we know, the Prevention Zone is only as good as your implementation of safety awareness strategies. What I am referring to is the basic fact that no matter how many security devices you have, they are not worth a thing if, through poor personal safety habits, you let a criminal into your home. Let us talk about your plans to prevent this from happening in the first place.

Basic Principles.

The four basic principles to guide you in safety awareness are:
1. Give out as little information as possible.
about yourself (and your family).
2. Be alert for scams, trickery, and targeting.
3. Utilize your security devices.
4. Plan for an emergency.

Telephone Safety Strategies

The telephone is a way for a criminal to gain information about you. How you are listed, how your phone is answered, and the information given out on the phone can provide either little information or lots of information about you and your activities.

Listings

If you choose to list your telephone number, list your first two initials and your last name. You can opt for an unlisted number or a fictitious name. Do not list your address. Street address directories, sometimes called reverse directories list street addresses, name, and telephone number. These directories are used by sales and marketing people (and criminals). I suggest that you call the telephone company, and make sure that your name either is not listed or is removed from the street address directory.

Taking Calls

Be cautious about what you say on the phone. Although a stranger may, of course, phone for a legitimate purpose, he may also phone to find out if you live alone or if you are at home. He may call to harass you or for some other criminal purpose. Never give any personal information on the phone to someone you do not know or trust. If the caller asks for the man of the house just state that he is unable to come to the phone and offer to have the call returned. The same procedure applies when you are unsure about the legitimacy of any call. Tell the caller that it is inconvenient for you to speak just then and offer to return the call. If you choose to return the call, check on the legitimacy of the number.

Obscene or Harassing Calls

If you receive either obscene or harassing phone calls, it is best to hang up immediately. If the calls persist, continue the procedure of hanging up and file a report with the police. Then notify the telephone company and ask to speak to the specialist who handles these types of calls. Obscene and harassing phone calls are prohibited by federal and state laws. You may request to have your number changed at no charge or ask the phone company to put a trap on the line. They may request that you keep a log of the obscene or harassing calls for a week or two.

Telephone Answering Machines

Your goal here is to minimize your risk of the caller guessing that you are not at home. Therefore, leave a message that gives as little information as possible about you or your whereabouts. An example of this is, "We are unable to come to the phone right now. Please leave your name, number, and message and we will get back to you as soon as possible." You may also use a telephone answering machine to screen your calls.

Mailboxes and Rental Box Tips

Do not put your name, initials or any other identifying information on your mailbox. The post office delivers to the address, not the name. If you live in a rural area, I suggest that you obtain a post office box, and not have anything valuable sent to your home address. Thieves steal from mailboxes. Even if you don't live in a rural area, you may want to consider obtaining a P.O. box. You could also choose to rent a box at one of the mail rental companies. This way, you would have a different mailing address, which is a street address. This way, you can also list your personal checks, drivers' license and car registration with this rental address. This helps in preserving your privacy.

Personal Check Security

Checks go through many hands, and provide much information about you. Your goal is to provide as little as possible. Have your first two initials and last name on your personal checks. List either a post office box or your work address on the check. Do not list your home telephone number, use your work number or another number, but not your home number.

Front Door Safety

You are not legally or morally obligated to answer your door or let someone in—including the police. The police can enter against your wishes only if they have a warrant or if they have reason to believe that a crime is being committed. You have the right to see the warrant and demand identification. Be very wary. Being alone with a stranger in your home is being in an extremely isolated, vulnerable position.

Be Assertive

Only let the person at the door in the house if you really wish to do so. You don't even have to answer the door if you don't wish to. When you answer the door, identify your caller to your satisfaction before permitting him or her to enter. First check through the peephole to see who it is. (If it is nighttime, either leave the porch light on, or have a photo-sensitive motion detector light which will turn on if someone comes to your door.) If you decide to answer the door, ask through the door who the person is and request proof of identification. Remember, chains are no barrier between you and the person at the door, so don't rely on one to protect you.

If you have a dog, keep it on a leash with you. If you lock the dog in a room or put it outside, it cannot help protect you. If the caller is at your door at an inconvenient time for you (you may be alone, for example,) give him no information but tell him that you will reschedule the visit at a more convenient time. Then, make the appointment for a time when you are not alone. Above all, don't feel that you have to let the person into your home. Your sense of well-being and safety is more important than his time.

Close Your Drapes

Go outside your home at night and see what you can find out about those inside. It is important to take precautions so that no one can see in. Make sure that your window coverings afford privacy, and close them at night.

Bragging or Talking

Outdoors Near Your Home

Keep information about your home, your plans, your possessions and your family quiet. You may want to call to a neighbor across the fence, and tell him, for example, that you are going on a trip next week. Don't. Speak to the neighbor indoors. You do not know who may be listening.

At the Grocery Store, Bank, or Hair Salon

These are examples of places to keep quiet about your personal life. If you must talk about a trip, for example, do so after you come back. As above, you do not know who may be listening.

Emergency Plans

The best way to handle an emergency is to plan in advance what you will do should a crisis situation arise. The following are some suggestions as to preventive measures you can begin to put into effect now.

Safe Room

It is a good idea to designate one room of your house as a safe room—usually your bedroom. It is where to go should an intruder break into your home. Since interior doors are very flimsy, the door to this room will have to be reinforced. Install a deadbolt lock, and if the door swings outward, pin the hinges (See Figure 64. Securing a door with outside hinges). Make sure that the windows to this room are secure, but that you have an escape exit. If you are on the second floor or above, have a fire ladder (chain ladder) available. This ladder will serve a dual purpose.

This safe room should have a cellular phone or a C.B. radio, which wouldn't be affected if your phone lines were out. If you have a portable cellular phone for your car, you can bring it into your bedroom at night.

Make sure to keep your house alarm system, or portable alarm system for this room, armed.

Secret Code Words

Consider establishing a special secret code word or sentence with members of your family or trusted friends. You could use this word or sentence to warn someone of danger or to let them know that you are in danger and to get help immediately. If an intruder is in your home and has come face to face with you, you may be able to convince him that someone is expecting your phone call. You could then make a phone call and leave your secret message. Such a code message could be: "Call the pharmacist to fill my prescription." Translation: "Call the police!"

Confronting an Intruder

If you hear a break-in

If you hear someone breaking into your home, leave if doing so is safe (take your phone with you). As soon as you are safely outside, immediately call the police.

If you come home and find that someone has broken in, don't go in. You don't want to surprise a burglar or block his escape route, he may become violent. Go to a neighbor's house or the nearest phone and call the police.

If you come face to face with an intruder

What if you come face to face with an intruder in your home? The answer is, what is more important, you or your property? I would suggest that you try to stay cool, ask the burglar what he wants, and cooperate with him only as long as your bodily safety is not being threatened. If you consider that he is threatening you with bodily injury or rape, fight back, if feasible, to incapacitate him and then get out of the house and call the police.

Telephoning for help

The police will give immediate priority to a call reporting a crime in progress or bodily injury. When you call the police in an emergency situation, make sure to let them know that it is an emergency and tell them clearly what is happening. If an intruder is in your house or you hear someone trying to break in, make sure that the police understand that the crime is in progress. Give them the location, your phone number, your name (if you wish) and any description of the individual or weapons he may have. Try to stay as calm as possible.

Good Neighbors

Good neighbors can help one another in many ways to prevent crime. A neighbor can watch your home while you are away for the day or a longer time. A neighbor can keep your spare key for you. This is much wiser than placing it under the welcome mat or in the mailbox.

Neighborhood groups or block clubs can significantly reduce the incidence of crime on the block. They are often organized with the assistance of the local police department, which provides technical advice on crime prevention. Neighbors meet about once a month. They cooperate to report suspicious activities, to keep an eye on homes when the residents are away, and to learn personal and property safeguards. Members of the group put warning decals on their doors and windows, notifying potential intruders that their premises are being watched.

Some neighborhood groups, especially in inner cities, have developed a whistle system. Neighbors carry whistles on their keychains to blow when in trouble, when hearing someone else blowing his or her whistle, or when they find someone acting suspiciously.

Key Points to Remember

1. Give out as little information as possible about yourself (and your family).

2. Be alert for scams, trickery and targeting.

3. You are not obligated to answer your door or let someone in.

4. Utilize your security devices.

5. Plan for an emergency.

LESSON SEVENTEEN
On The Road—Travel Safety

Before You Leave

Make your home look lived in. If a potential intruder can tell from looking or calling you on the phone that nobody is home, then your home is a target. Therefore, before you go on a trip (or even leave for the day,) it is essential that you take certain steps so that your home has the appearance of being occupied. In LESSONS FOURTEEN and SIXTEEN we discussed home security, including locks, locking devices, lighting, timers, window coverings, and alarms. We also discussed the psychological aspects of prevention. Please refer to these lessons for specifics on these devices and their use.

If You Leave Your Car at Home

If you leave your car at home, have a neighbor move it on a regular basis. If this is not possible, lock the car and keep it in the garage. You might ask a neighbor, who owns more than one car to park his/her car in your driveway while you are away.

Services

I do not believe in notifying service agencies that you will be away. You never know who might be gathering this information. Instead, ask a friend or your good neighbor (See LESSON SIXTEEN) to pick up your newspaper or anything else that is thrown on your lawn. You might also ask your neighbor to fill your trash can, and take in your mail. You might even have an arrangement with your neighbor to open and close your drapes. Arrange to have your lawn mowed or sidewalk shoveled. If you have pets, arrange to have a friend come and feed and walk them, if appropriate. Animals are happier at home and dogs, especially, can offer a measure of protection if an intruder approaches the home.

Planning for Security

Tell as few people as possible that you will be away. Make sure that you do not make any announcements that you will be gone. Leave your itinerary and telephone numbers with a trusted individual so you can be reached in case of an emergency. Plan to check back with this person at periodic intervals.

Advance Planning

Earlier, in the discussion on streetwise safety strategies, I emphasized the importance of knowing your routes, locations of police and fire stations, and places where you could go for assistance. The same preparation applies when you travel. As a stranger, you are not as comfortable and sure of yourself as someone who lives in the area. If you are lost or look lost, your body language will indicate this. Therefore, in planning your trip, get as much information as possible ahead of time about the places you will be visiting. A street map of any city you plan to visit will help. Become familiar with it. Locate the hotel or motel where you will be staying, the places you will be visiting, and the locations of police stations. It also may be wise to speak to a travel agent or people who have been to the area. Travel books can also be useful.

If you are staying at hotels or motels, guarantee the rooms ahead of time with a credit card. This way you will make sure your room is waiting for you when you arrive, no matter how late. You can also specify that you do not want an adjoining room.

Money and Documents

Carry limited amounts of cash. Purchase recognized travelers checks a few days before you leave. You also may wish to carry a couple of credit cards. Take appropriate identification and health insurance information with you, but restrict your documentation to the minimum. Make sure you make a record of what you have taken with you. The best way to do this is to go to a photocopy machine and make copies of the documents you will take with you. I also suggest that you list who and where to notify in case of loss next to the copy of the document. Also remember to take a list of important phone numbers.

If You Take Your Car

Car safety and carjacking prevention were discussed in LESSON TWELVE. In this lesson, we will cover additional information for travel safety.

Pack your car in the garage, if possible. You don't want anyone to see that you are putting suitcases into your car and leaving. It is best to put most things in the trunk. If you car is out on the street, though, it is not wise to pack it up the night before. If you must pack a car on the street, try to be as quick and discreet as possible. Look before you pack. If you see a suspicious person or car, delay your packing until you feel more comfortable.

Make sure that your car is in good working order. Check to see that your spare tire has air, and that you have kept up on the maintenance schedule. Fill your tank with gas and check the oil level. Join an auto club (or put a rider on your home insurance policy), that provides for roadside service. Consider buying a C.B. radio or cellular phone so that you can call for help if you need it. Take emergency supplies with you. This includes food, water, a first aid kit, a flashlight, and a blanket.

If your car breaks down on the road, get out, raise the hood, and get back inside. Lock your doors and windows, and turn on the emergency flashers. Call for help on your cellular phone or C.B. radio. If you have a Call Police banner, put it on the windshield. Do not accept help from a stranger who stops and offers to assist you. You can tell him that the police have been called, or ask them to phone for assistance. Do not lower your window. Above all, do not get out of your car. If you have a flat tire, assess your situation. If it is not safe to change the tire, drive slowly on the shoulder until you get to an exit or a well-lighted business. You may ruin either the tire or rim, but that may be a wiser alternative than being stranded on the side of the road.

If You Rent a Car

First, check to make sure that the car is in good working order before you leave the lot. Check the fluid levels and the tire pressure. Be sure that the lights and turn signals are working. Make sure you understand how to operate all the controls. Remove any decals which identify the car as rented.

Know your routes. Check your maps before you leave the parking lot. You do not want to appear lost. Be aware. If you think that someone is following you, drive to the nearest police station, fire station, hospital emergency room, or open service station. Do not pick up hitchhikers (as well as never hitch-hike).

If You Take a Taxi

Do not give the driver any personal information about yourself. You want to appear that you know what you are doing and where you are going—as opposed to being a stranger, alone and unfamiliar with the area. Have an idea in advance of your route, and ask the driver for an estimate of the fare in advance. To make the driver as accountable as possible, note his name and license, write it down, and ask for a receipt.

If You Travel by Air

Take as little luggage as possible on your trip. It is best to take carry-on so that you can have control over your bags, and that you are not encumbered with too much luggage. This will also preclude the possibility of the luggage being lost, opened, or stolen before you claim it. Luggage with wheels are a good investment, or you can purchase a collapsible luggage cart. Make sure that you have good locks on your suitcases, and they are attended by you at all times. If you have a hold-over at the airport, use coin-operated lockers. Guard your tickets and purse or briefcase. If you require help with your bags, summon a skycap.

Hotel and Motel Security

Your hotel/motel security plan has three objectives—to safeguard yourself, to safeguard your valuables, and to prevent intruders from entering your room.

Checking In

When you check in, do so by first two initials and last name. Give your business address on the registration card, rather than your home address. If the hotel uses traditional keys, ask for all of them (for security purposes). Many times hotel clerks will give the key to a room to anyone who comes to the desk and asks for it. Volunteer or give out absolutely no personal information about yourself or your plans. If you are staying at a motel, make sure that your room is not on ground level, as these rooms are more vulnerable to intrusion.

Before you accept the room that the clerk assigned to you, ask to see it. Check to make sure that the locks work on the windows and/or sliding glass door. Request and check to see that it is not an adjoining room. Also, make sure that all amenities work, so that you do not have to call for someone to come in to fix anything. Also, check to be sure that the room is in a well-travelled area, rather than at the end of a dark, long hallway.

Portable Alarms

When I travel, I carry two portable alarms with me. One is a portable personal alarm, and the other is a portable motion detector alarm (Figure 71). This type of alarm will protect an area—such as a sliding glass door, window, or space. If anyone enters the room, within the range of the alarm, a loud siren will sound. Some personal alarms (Figure 72) can be attached to a specific door, such as the room door or adjoining door (if I have not been able to avoid a room that has one).

FIGURE 71. Interfear™ motion detector alarm
(Courtesy Professional Safety Inc.)

FIGURE 72. the Yelper™ personal alarm
(Courtesy Professional Safety Inc.)

Do Not Leave Anything of Value in the Room

Lock your suitcases before you leave, and put them away. Any small items of value that you do not want to take with you can usually be locked in a safe. Many rooms come with portable safes.

When You Leave the Room

Leave either the radio or television on. You want to give the impression that someone is in the room. Lock your door whenever you leave the room—even if it is only to go down the hall to use the ice machine.

Key Points to Remember

1. Plan for security. Tell as few people as possible that you will be away.

2. Make your home look lived in while you are away.

3. Utilize a good neighbor policy rather than cancelling services.

4. Make sure your car is in good working order.

5. Plan your trip ahead of time. Gather as much information as possible.

6. Pack for security.

7. Take portable alarms with you. You can use them on the street or for extra security in your room.

8. Your hotel/motel security plan has three objectives—to safeguard yourself, to safeguard your valuables, and to prevent intruders from entering your room.

LESSON EIGHTEEN
Defense Against Weapons

The Weapons Question

The question that I am asked most frequently is: "What am I supposed to do if someone threatens me with a knife or gun?" Your strategy, tactics, and response depend on the circumstances. Therefore, we will go through a series of scenarios and will discuss possible responses. Remember, I am only giving you suggestions so that you can prepare for a crisis situation. You choose what to do or not to do, based on your own best judgment of the situation.

Prevention

Prevention is always your best defense. In LESSON TWELVE—Streetwise Safety Strategies, we discussed the concepts of how not to be targeted in public—by keeping alert at all times and by developing street smarts. Since most assailants target people who are unaware, keep aware and send out alert body language—that you know where you are going, you know what you are doing, and that you respect yourself. If you consider the situation to be dangerous, you send out *don't mess with me!* signals (See LESSON THREE, How To Win—The Psychology of Fighting Back). If you seriously practice these safety awareness strategies, you will avoid most knife attacks and, indeed, most attacks.

Location of Attacker
Attacker at a Distance

Suppose you are in a parking garage or parking lot and an assailant, armed with a handgun, threatens you from a distance away. Your best strategy is to run away—fast! To make yourself less of a target, run in a zigzag pattern rather than in a straight line.

Threatened at Close Range

Your guiding principle is not to become intimidated. You need to stay calm, keep breathing, and be determined to get away at first chance. In many cases, you must create the opportunity to get away.

If you are threatened at close range by an armed assailant, assess the situation. Does he really have a weapon? Is it a robbery? Does he want you?

If the assailant claims to have a lethal weapon, calmly ask to see it. While this may seem unthinkable at first, the fact is that many women are raped by men who intimidate them with nonexistent weapons.

If the Assailant Produces a Weapon

This is one of the very few times that I do not recommend the strategy of immediately fighting back by raging (See Principles of Fighting in LESSON FIVE). What you need to do is to stay calm and keep breathing. If he wants money or your valuables, calmly give them to him. Remember, you cannot be replaced, and you are certainly more valuable than any possession that you have. You might want to consider using the dog and biscuit tactic. If you offer a dog a biscuit, and slowly take it out of the box, the dog will look at the biscuit. In this case, slowly take your wallet out of your purse or pocket— stating in a calm voice, "I am taking my wallet out of my purse (or back pocket)." The criminal's eyes will focus on this object. You then gently toss the wallet approximately a foot away. As criminal looks at the wallet, you run the other way.

Assailant Tries to Force You Into Automobile

You do not go. It is too dangerous to be taken off in an automobile with a rapist/kidnapper/murderer! These criminals try to get you off to an isolated area so that they can do what they want to you. I have thought for a long time how to say "No!" to a man with a gun. I believe that the best thing to do is to pretend to faint, if you are a woman. Men can pretend to have a heart attack. When you faint, you become an extremely heavy weight on the ground. It is extremely difficult, if not impossible, for a man with one available arm, to drag you into a car. If you feel two hands on you, then the gun is not pointing at you. You then immediately transform into your raging self, and viciously attack the attacker.

Armed Assailant Tries to Sexually Assault You

If a gun or knife is pointed at you, you may have to play along and pretend to do what the assailant wants for a while. Stay calm, continue to breathe, and tell yourself that he is going to make a mistake. Try to let him think that you are intimidated, and trick him into putting the weapon down. Then, as above, transform into your raging self, and viciously attack the attacker.

Knife Defenses

The time that you do not have a choice as to whether to fight back or not is when someone is actually attacking you with a knife. Here your goal is to prevent the knife from harming you, and then to incapacitate the attacker. We will deal with two types of attacks: the underhand thrusting attack and the overhand attack. The descriptions that follow are given for a right-handed attack. The left-handed attack will require using the opposite arm and moving to the opposite side from that described.

Caution: Knife defense skills are more advanced than previous skills. If you wish to use them, they require repeated practice, until you become proficient in their use.

Knife Defense—Underhand Thrusting Attack

Ascertain the direction of the attack. The principle in avoidance is to move your body out of the line of attack and to control the knife arm.

Attack to middle or right side

1. As the knife is thrust at you. sidestep to your left. This is to prevent you from being hit with the knife because you literally move your stomach out of the way.

2. At the same time, grab the side of the assailant's knife wrist with your right hand.

3. Immediately incapacitate the attacker by kicking him through the kneecap (Figure 75).

Attack to left side

1. As the knife is thrust at you (Figure 73), sidestep to your right. This is to prevent you from being hit with the knife because you literally move your stomach out of the way.

2. At the same time, grab the side of the assailant's knife wrist with your left hand (Figure 74).

3. Immediately incapacitate the attacker by kicking him through the kneecap (Figure 75).

FIGURE 73. (left) Knife defense, underhand thrusting attack
  FIGURE 74. (right) Knife defense, underhand thrusting attack: grab

FIGURE 75. Knife defense, underhand thrusting attack: kick

Knife Defense—Overhand Attack
Attack to middle or right side

1. As the assailant thrusts the knife at you, get into your stance (as if you had just punched—see Figure 7). It is extremely important to assume the correct stance position. This will give you the power to break the thrust of the attack.

2. At the same time, straighten and thrust out your right arm, grabbing the knife wrist.

3. Immediately incapacitate the attacker by kicking him through the kneecap (Figure 77).

Attack to left side

1. As the assailant thrusts the knife at you, get into your stance (as if you had just punched—see Figure 7). It is extremely important to assume the correct stance position. This will give you the power to break the thrust of the attack.

2. At the same time, straighten and thrust out your left arm, grabbing the knife wrist (Figure 76).

3. Immediately incapacitate the attacker by kicking him through the kneecap (Figure 77).

FIGURE 76. Knife defense, overhand attack: wrist grab

FIGURE 77. Knife defense, overhand attack: kick

Practice Drill

Purchase a toy rubber knife to practice knife defenses. Start slowly, then increase your speed. Take the time to focus on your partner's attack. You will then have plenty of time to respond.

Key Points to Remember

1. The best defense against knife attacks is prevention. By being aware and alert, you will prevent most assaults from occurring in the first place.

2. You are much more important than valuables or cash. It is better to cooperate with an armed robber.

3. If the attacker's goal is to harm you, then your decision, in most cases, is to fight back. When you choose to fight back, and how, depends on circumstances.

4. Do not, in any case, be taken off in a car with an assailant.

5. If attacked with a knife, your goal is to move out of the way, control the knife arm, and incapacitate the assailant.

LESSON NINETEEN
Physical Defense—Self-Defense Weapons

Guns as Self-Defense Weapons

The issue of whether to purchase a gun for self-defense is discussed extensively in Chapter Nine of *Exploding the Myth of Self-Defense*. Topics discussed include: The growth of female handgun ownership; guns and self-defense; the availability of handguns for self-defense; and the dangers of having a gun in the home. Owning a gun is a personal choice. Before you even consider carrying a handgun for self-defense, or keeping one in the home, check on your local laws for the legalities.

I would definitely caution against keeping a handgun in the home if: (1) there are children in the home, (2) a member of the household has a tendency toward depression, or (3) anyone in the household has a bad temper. What I found, after reviewing the statistics, is that no matter how much of an equalizer a gun is and no matter how powerful it may make you feel, under the circumstances mentioned above, the numbers overwhelmingly indicate that the dangers of having a gun in the home outweigh the benefits.

Tear Gas and O.C. (Pepper)

Tear gas is a non-lethal self-defense weapon. When used properly, it can incapacitate an assailant for approximately fifteen minutes, giving you a good chance to get safely away. What it is designed to do is to temporarily blind the assailant. Tear gas also causes a stinging and burning sensation on the skin, coughing and sneezing, and difficulty in breathing.

If you choose to carry tear gas or any other weapon for self-defense, you must understand how to carry it and how to use it for self-defense. It is also important for you to have information on how to choose a canister. (Chapter Nine of *Exploding the Myth of Self-Defense* discusses in detail the differences between the three defense sprays.) Check your local laws on the legality of carrying tear gas or any other weapons for self-defense. Also note that it is illegal to take tear gas aboard an aircraft (either check-in or in the cabin).

How to choose a canister

All forms of tear gas work within two to three seconds when fired in the open eyes of an assailant. Part of your choice depends on the chemical itself, and part depends on its delivery system.

C.N. (commonly known as mace) is the weakest and least effective form of tear gas. Its main drawback is that it works on the nerve centers of the body that control pain. If those nerve centers are depressed, it may not work. Therefore, C.N. may not work if someone is drunk, under the influence of drugs, is agitated or angry.

C.S. (commonly known as military tear gas) is a much stronger, more punishing chemical agent than C.N. It works on most assailants. Be cautioned, though, that C.S. does not vaporize as rapidly as mace. Therefore, it is best to purchase a canister which shoots out as a spray or has a gunshot pattern, rather than a stream. This way, even if the assailant is wearing glasses, the tear gas will affect his eyes.

O.C. (commonly known as pepper gas or spray) is the third type of self-defense spray on the market. It is a strong inflammatory agent. However, it is the least volatile of the three and requires a delivery system which spreads (such as a fogger or spray).

How to Carry Tear Gas

If you want to count on tear gas to help you in self-defense, you must have it with you and available all the time. At night, it is by your bedside. On the streets, depending on your perceived level of danger, you carry it in your hand, put it on your belt or waistband, or carry it in your pocket. When you are indoors at work, for example, keep it in your purse or briefcase. I suggest utilizing a detachable keyring to attach it to a loop of your purse or briefcase. That way it does not descend into the black hole. When you leave for the day, detach the canister and carry it with you as described above.

How to Use Tear Gas for Self-defense

Hold the canister with your thumb on the trigger (See Figure 78). Get into your stance, yell at the assailant, and spray directly into his face. Your primary target is his eyes. Your secondary target is his mouth. Depending on the range of the canister, the average effective distance is about ten feet. Use plenty of the chemical, and keep shooting until the assailant either drops to the ground screaming in pain or runs off screaming.

FIGURE 78. How to hold a tear gas canister

First Aid

If you accidently get some spray on you, wash your eyes copiously with cool water. Rinse your face with cool water. You might also try baking soda and water on your skin (not your eyes) if you are affected by C.S. Do not rub. Fresh air or fanning the area will also help.

Maintaining Your Canister

Check your canister for pressure when you get it. You do this by giving it a half a second burst. Then, check the canister for pressure every four to six months. If the canister leaks, you will know it. If so, immediately seal it in a plastic zip lock bag. A good shelf life for most canisters is two to two and a half years.

Stun Guns

Stun guns are highly effective, underrated self-defense weapons (see Figure 80.) They deliver anywhere from 35,000 to 150,000 volts of power, yet are non-lethal because there amperage is very low (no more than .6 amps.) You can use a stun gun two ways against an assailant. The first way is psychological. When threatened with attack, get into your stance, aim the stun gun at the assailant, yell, and press the trigger (on/off switch). A loud crackling blue bolt of lightening will cross the test arc. Many times this is enough to scare away the attacker.

The second way to stop the assailant is by physically disabling him. To do this, shove the contact probes into the assailant, while pressing on the trigger. The jolt goes through clothing, and his muscles collapse. If he grabs you while you are firing the stun gun it doesn't matter since the charge will flow directly into him and not back to you. Try to ram the stun gun into the assailant for several seconds. He will drop down screaming in pain.

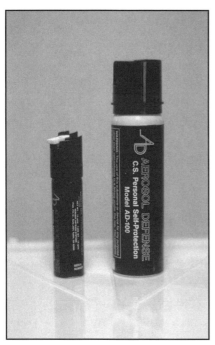

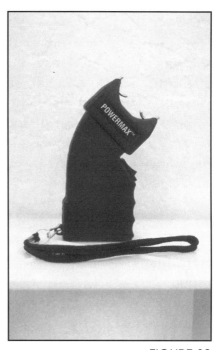

FIGURE 79.
Aerosol Defense™ Tear Gas
(Courtesy Aerosol Defense
Industries)

FIGURE 80.
Powermax™ Stun Gun
(Courtesy Marshall & Johnson)

Stun Gun or Tear Gas?

Why pick one weapon over another. One reason is personal preference. Tear gas can stop an assailant at about ten feet away. The stun gun can scare an assailant off, but to stop him, you must make physical contact. I personally have both. I carry tear gas with me all the time except when I travel by plane. In this case, I take a stun gun. If you want to take a stun gun on a plane, take the battery out (it works on a nine volt alkaline battery) and put the stun gun in your checked-in luggage. You may not legally bring a stun gun in the cabin of the plane.

Personal Alarms

While not classified as weapons, personal alarms can serve a dual purpose for self-defense (See Figure 72). If threatened with attack, you can set off the alarm. A very loud ear piercing sound will disorient the potential attacker and may bring attention to him. Remember though, that noise is just part of your defense. Loud noise combined with physical resistance and running away are the best and most effective strategies.

Alarms are also used as warning devices so that you are not taken by surprise. On the streets, awareness keeps you out of harm's way. When you cannot be aware, an alarm can warn you of danger, and also scare off a potential intruder (See (Figure 71).

Many alarms are on the market. They range from a simple old fashioned whistle to battery powered multi-purpose portable alarms. You have a broad range of choices to investigate.

Key Points to Remember

1. Tear gas is a non-lethal self-defense weapon which can incapacitate an assailant for approximately fifteen minutes.

2. Stun guns are highly effective self-defense weapons which deliver anywhere from 35,000 to 150,000 volts of power, yet are not lethal because the amperage is too low.

3. Alarms can be part of your defense strategies when combined with physical resistance and running away.

LESSON TWENTY
Putting It All Together

The last day of class, I ask my students to share with the class how each of them feels now compared to the first day of class. Lori, a recent participant, had the following to say.

"I was so afraid. Incidents of sexual harassment and assault left me paralyzed with fear. I stayed in my apartment so that no one could hurt me, but my anxiety became so great that I couldn't feel safe even at home. I felt powerless and trapped. I thought of taking a self-defense class. ...After two years of therapy, I was ready to take this step.

"...I didn't know what to expect when I entered the first class meeting, but as Judith spoke, I knew I had come to the right place. She was saying things that I have been wanting to hear for years: I didn't have to be afraid anymore: I could learn to empower myself; I shouldn't blame myself or feel guilty for the things that have happened to me. I'm a survivor, and coming to her class meant that I was doing something positive to take care of myself.

"Judith was speaking to everyone but her words touched me deeply. I cried through that first class, relieved that I wasn't alone in my struggle and hopeful for change. After class I wanted to thank Judith and tell her how happy I was to be in her class, but I couldn't get the words out. She understood and was very supportive. She gave me a special reading assignment: the success stories of the women in her past self-defense classes [Chapter Three of *Exploding the Myth of Self-Defense*].

"...When I got Judith's book, *Exploding the Myth of Self-Defense*, I read it from cover to cover. My highliter pen ran out of ink because so many things in her book spoke to me. One quote in particular stands out: 'Personal power means control of your choices, control of your life—not permitting anyone to take away your integrity as a human being.' I found that these words applied not only to taking care of myself on the streets, but to my life in general as well. What I have learned in class and in the reading has spilled over into other areas of my life. ...I have been able to make some very positive decisions and changes in my life.

"...I feel that all women should know about the physical and psychological skills that Dr. Judith Fein teaches in her self-defense classes. It is as if she has let me in on a big secret. She has helped me to find something that I had hidden deep within me. Because of what she has taught me...my world has become so much bigger, and with both arms flung wide, I can reach out to embrace all that I can be and all that I will be."

INDEX

R

Rape resistance
  acquaintance rape   82-84
  effective strategies   72. 84-86
  ineffective strategies   72
  stranger rape   71–72

S

Security check   126
Self-defense   18
  as survival skills   18
  joy of self-defense   19
Self-esteem   19, 95
Stance   54. *See also* Fighting skills
Street harassment   111-112
Stun guns   168–169
Street smarts. *See* Prevention

T

Tear gas/pepper
  First aid   168
  How to carry tear gas   167
  How to choose a canister   166
  How to use tear gas for self-defense   167
Telephone safety strategies   141-143
Travel safety
  advance planning   150
  hotel and motel security   153-154
  money and documents   151

V

Victimization
  blaming   33
  victim behavior   74-75
Video inventory   128

W

Weapons
  armed assailant   158-159
  physical resistance   73
  prevention   157
Windows   131-132

Y

Yelling   28-30

ORDER FORM

Books/Cassettes

HOW TO ORDER

- Phone Orders (Visa/Mastercard):
  Call toll-free: 1-800-437-2338
- FAX Orders (Visa/Mastercard): (707) 823-3581
- Postal Orders: Fill in coupon below and send to:
  Torrance Publishing Company
  P.O. Box 2558
  Sebastopol, CA 95473

- **EXPLODING THE MYTH OF SELF-DEFENSE** by Judith Fein, Ph.D.
  Audiocassette: $16.95
  Dr. Judith Fein breaks new ground in the philosophy behind—
  and strategies for—self-defense for women. "Fein's book is a
  gift to women who want control over their lives." (Mary Ellen
  Sullivan, Booklist, American Library Association)
- **HOW TO FIGHT BACK AND WIN—The Joy of Self-Defense**
  by Judith Fein: $21.95
- **FEMALINES** by Nancy Worthington: $23.95
  A book of intriguing transformations and metamorphoses
  between cats and women through text and original artworks

Item	Quantity	Price Each	Tax*	Total
		Shipping		$4.95

Please ship to:
Name _____
Address_____ City_____
State_____ Zip_____ Telephone_____
Check enclosed ☐   or charge my VISA/Mastercard ☐
Card No._____ Expriation date_____

*CA residents only add 7.5% tax   Signature _____